# Ancestral Tales

An anthology of sea yarns,
life stories and memoirs

# Ancestral Tales

An anthology of sea yarns,
life stories and memoirs

collated by
J Pigott

© Janet Pigott, 2012

Published by P J Publications

www.janetpigott.co.uk

All rights reserved. No part of this book may be reproduced, adapted, stored in a retrieval system or transmitted by any means, electronic, mechanical, photocopying, or otherwise without the prior written permission of the author.

The rights of Janet Pigott to be identified as the author of this work have been asserted in accordance with the Copyright, Designs and Patents Act 1988.

A CIP catalogue record for this book is available from the British Library.

ISBN 978-0-9566761-1-5

Book and cover design by Clare Brayshaw

Prepared and printed by:

York Publishing Services Ltd
64 Hallfield Road
Layerthorpe
York YO31 7ZQ

Tel: 01904 431213

Website: www.yps-publishing.co.uk

# DEDICATION

*For the families of the authors, who have inherited the life-stories and tales from their antecedents.*

# PREVIOUS PUBLICATIONS

WORD PROCESSING EXPERIENCE
(with co-author Roger Atkins-Green), 1982, STP Ltd.

WORD PROCESSING EXPERIENCE TEACHER'S EDITION
1983, STP Ltd.

WORDSTAR™ COMMANDS CONVERSION KIT
1983, STP Ltd.

OFFICE PROOFREADING
(with co-author Marion Smith), 1986, STP Ltd.

KEYBOARDING PRACTICE, 1986, WTC

'IT' TAKES A WOMAN
2010, PJ Publications, YPS-Books Ltd

REPORTS AND SHORT STORIES IN:

Office Skills Magazine, 1984, Pitman

A Little Book of Smells, 2008, Pens of Erdington, Roaring Greasepaint

Chores – The Truth about Housework, 2010, Pens of Erdington, Roaring Greasepaint, Lulu.com

# CONTENTS

ACKNOWLEDGEMENTS ... ix

PHOTOGRAPHS OF THE AUTHORS ... xi

EXTRACT FROM THE PRITCHARD FAMILY TREE ... xiv

STORIES FROM TALL SHIPS
 BY FREDERICK OSCAR FINLAYSON
   Introduction to sea stories of the 1800's ... 1
   1 ~ A Hero ... 3
   2 ~ Aboard the Russell Castle ... 5
   3 ~ Surprises all round ... 8
   4 ~ The Island of Malakula ... 10
   5 ~ Happenings in Tanna ... 12
   6 ~ The First White Man ... 14
   7 ~ A Leap in the Dark ... 16
   8 ~ Pigs at Sea ... 18
   9 ~ When I came home in 1870 ... 20

DEAR DOMINIC BY MARGARET COX
   Introduction to the letter written by an octogenarian
   to her grandson ... 27
   Dear Dominic ... 28

THE WILLIAM EDWARD MEAKIN STORY
 BY W E MEAKIN
   Introduction to the autobiography of a blacksmith
   and remarkable Army farrier ... 57
   The William Edward Meakin Story ... 59

MEMBERS OF THE PRITCHARD FAMIY
PHOTOGRAPHS ... 103

A BYGONE ERA  BY VIOLET TAYLOR
    Introduction to the recollections of the daughter
    of a publican      107
    A Bygone Era      108

CROSSING THE CLASS DIVIDE?
THE ENIGMA OF MARGARET WILSON BROWN
BY MICHAEL (MIKE) RACE
    Introduction to the recollections of the Race family in York
    and a mystery surrounding a favourite aunt, by a family and
    oral historian      129
    Crossing The Class Divide?      130

TRUTH IS STRANGER THAN FICTION
BY JANET PIGOTT
    Introduction to memoirs by author J Pigott      145
    1 ~ A Terrified Trio      146
    2 ~ My First Memory      148
    3 ~ Childhood Memories      150
    4 ~ Holiday in Filey      154
    5 ~ A Day Out on my own      157
    6 ~ The Cardiac Machine      161
    7 ~ The Light in the Dark      163
    8 ~ A Misunderstanding in Verona      165
    9 ~ Eavesdropping      167
    10 ~ The Missing R      168
    11 ~ Mum's Routine Blood Pressure Check-up at
        the age of 98      172
    12 ~ My First Hip Operation      176

# ACKNOWLEDGEMENTS

I am indebted to my family members and people who have encouraged me to compile this anthology of tales, fables yarns and short stories from times past, and given me photographs.

Although all the following people mentioned in this paragraph are no longer with us, I give thanks to my Great-grandfather, Frederick Oscar Finlayson ('FOF'), his niece Nora Williams, for recording his tales in shorthand and typing them out, and her daughter, Eileen Hillary, for donating the transcriptions to me. I think the stories give a good start to this book and provide opportunities for further research to anyone interested in surfing the 'net for evidence of any realism in them.

Distant cousins, Mike Race and John Cox, were instrumental in setting me off on a career in creative writing when I retired from employment at the end of 1999, by loaning me a handwritten copy of *Margaret Cox's Diary Pages*. I was amazed and impressed with the quality of Margaret's writing when she was in her eighties, and her life-story inspired me to put pen to paper as a future hobby. To John and Dominic his son thank you both, for your kindness and generosity in letting me include Margaret's life story in this publication; and to the late Margaret I give my thanks for the wonderful memories you so lucidly recorded for your family at the age of 83.

In 2011, when I was rummaging through some old photographs I came across one of a young woman that I'd never seen before. No one in my family recognised her, so I posted a copy to another cousin, Derek Meakin, to see if he could help. He did. He identified the subject as my Mum, aged 23, from a similar one inherited from his Mum, Evie Meakin, my mother's elder sister. He also sent me lots of family photographs which I'd never seen before, and a copy of his Dad's life story found after his Dad had died. This had been written on little scraps of numbered paper. To my modest Uncle, the late William Meakin, and my cousin Derek, thank you for sharing these memories, and giving me permission to include this wonderful autobiography of growing up to be a blacksmith and Army farrier.

My Mum, the late Violet Taylor (née Pritchard), was a happy soul; the lynch-pin of her family. She loved to recall her youth and recorded some of it onto audio tapes for York Oral History Society when she was in her nineties. She had a remarkable memory of times past and for people's names and dates. Thank you, Mum, for all your care over the years, your interest in our well-being, and your attention to detail in your yarns.

My cousin, Mike Race, has mentored me through my creative writing career after I left work. He has helped and guided me beyond belief. Thank You, Mike, for all the help and encouragement you have given me over the past decade; for reading large sections of the text of this book, and for the story and photographs you have provided. I truly value your excellent contributions.

York author Van Wilson very kindly proofread the Bygone Era section of the book and put me right on the spellings of several trade names. Her eagle eye also found some typing errors, and I am extremely grateful to her for drawing my attention to these. Thank you very much for your help, Van.

My thanks are also given to Andrew Macklewain Cross, Proprietor of the Black Swan for two pictures of the Leeds Arms, which at one time was attached to his property.

I am appreciative of the work done by Clare Brayshaw, Book Designer, and the entire team at YPS. Thank you, Duncan, for your personal welcome and giving me the opportunity to see these stories in print. Your staff have done an excellent job. I thank everyone involved in this production and forthcoming sales.

Most of all, I owe a huge debt of gratitude to my dear husband, Peter Pigott. His diligent research verifying Family History dates and names has been invaluable, as has his tolerance and patience with me over the time I've spent at my computer. Thank you, Peter, for all your dedication in checking facts for me. You are an absolute gem.

**Janet Pigott**

October 2011

# PHOTOGRAPHS OF THE AUTHORS OF THE STORIES

Frederick Oscar Finlayson

Margaret Cox (née Kilcullen)

William Edward Meakin

Violet Taylor (née Pritchard)

Frederick Oscar Finlayson
Aged 91

Margaret Cox
Aged about 40

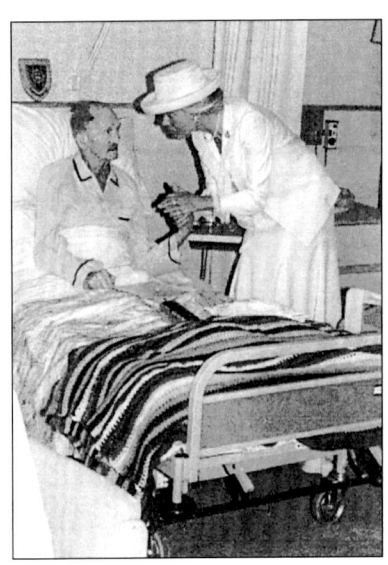

William Meakin
Aged 85

Violet Taylor (née Pritchard)
Aged 89

Mike Race, Chairman, York
Oral History Society

Margaret Race
Aged about 40

John Cox
Aged about 20

Derek Meakin
Aged 74

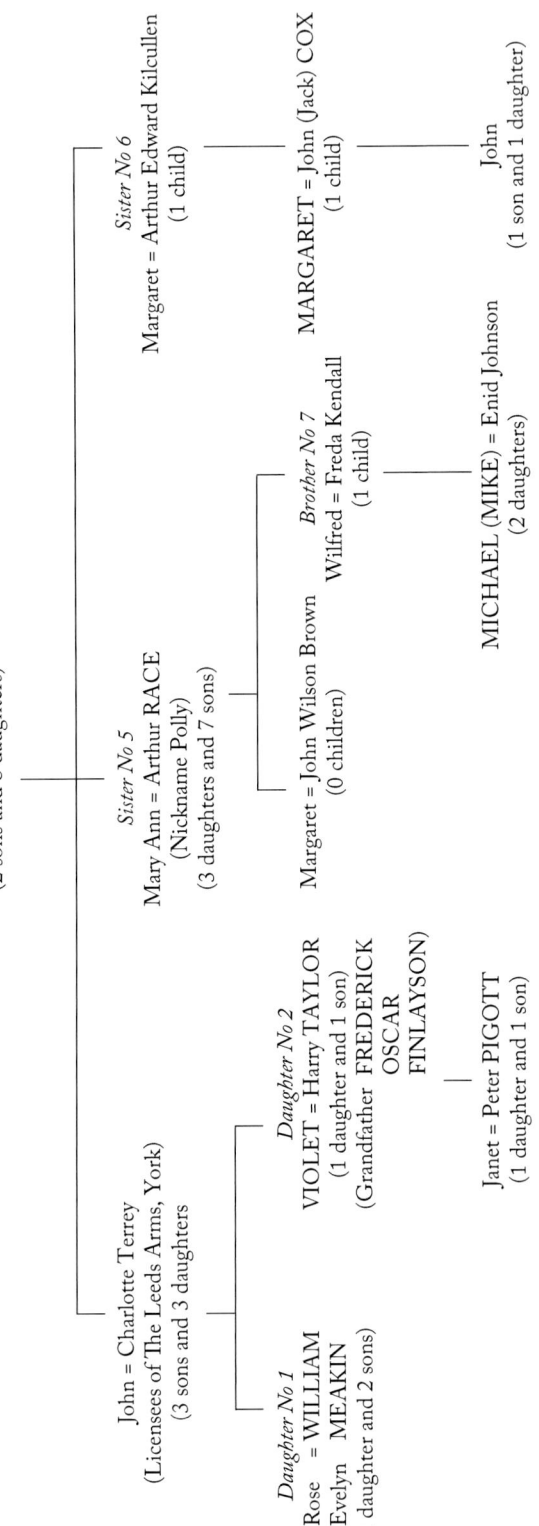

# STORIES FROM TALL SHIPS
## BY
## FREDERICK OSCAR FINLAYSON

Frederick Oscar Finlayson, aged 95

# INTRODUCTION

My dear Aunt Maisie (Mabel Taylor), is buried in Gateshead Cemetery with her parents and grandparents. Her wonderful father, my grandfather Henry Taylor, was a Chief Engineer in the Merchant Navy. He was a lovely man in every way and all the members of our family loved him dearly. But the fascinating character who lays below him is my Great-grandfather, Frederick Oscar Finlayson, affectionately referred to in the family as 'FOF' or Pa.

When I was growing up in the 1940's FOF was coming to the end of his life, but I remember him well. He was 91 when I was born and lived a further five years.

FOF was born in 1848 and died in 1944, aged 96 years. He left behind photographs and stories which I inherited when my Aunt died in 1996. A suitcase containing unnamed and undated carte de visites and studio photographs has led to many years of Family History research (my husband's hobby) and when we realised there was a surviving member of FOF's niece's family, Eileen Hillary, living in Worthing, we contacted her and she invited us to visit her at the family home which she'd inherited from her mother, Nora Hillary née Williams.

Eileen told us that when she was a child she was a spastic from Poliomyelitis and was confined to a wheelchair. Her mother had married Andrew John Hillary in 1915 and they had lived and worked in London. Andrew Hillary died in 1927 and when Nora heard that "Mr Hitler" was intending to declare war on Britain, she moved to a new house being built in Worthing – to be further away from the City which was rumoured could be badly bombed – and the sea air would be fresher for her disabled daughter.

My husband and I visited Eileen, still living at 49 Pelham Road, Worthing, in 1996. We talked about our ancestors and she identified some of the people in the photographs. Eileen also gave us several pages of stories which her mother had typed from her verbatim shorthand.

These were sea yarns which FOF had told Eileen when they had visited him for a week's holiday in 1935. Every day "Uncle Fred" had told Eileen a tale of his times at sea when he was a young man. Nora was so impressed that she recorded them in shorthand and when they got home, transcribed them on an old manual typewriter, so that she could read them to Eileen many more times in the future. Eileen very kindly gave me the stories.

When I first read them, I recognised some of them as having been told to me in 1943 when I was staying with my grandparents in Newcastle-on-Tyne, and Great-grandpa (FOF) lived with them. I wasn't sure whether they were genuine or fictitious tales but my husband checked with Lloyds Register and found some of the ships named. After an initial flurry of research I lost interest in the yarns and filed the papers in a drawer together with a telescope that Eileen had given us as a keepsake memory of him.

In June 2011 I attended a writing retreat at Erdington Library in Birmingham. One of the sessions was designated to writing stories from old documents and we were asked to take along a birth, marriage or death certificate, or something interesting which an antecedent had written. I took FOF's stories.

One participant on the course was fascinated with my contribution and urged me to scan them into my computer and share them with the group. It was at that point that I wondered whether there was any truth in them or whether they were just an old seaman's fantasies.

I surfed the 'net to see if any of the ships were mentioned. I found them all. I also found information about the shipwreck of The Royal Charter and a detailed article about Guze Ruggier (Joe Rogers) the hero who was awarded the Royal National Lifeboat Institution Gold Medal in 1859, referred to in FOF's story "A Hero". I also found numerous references to the Scottish Missionary John Gibson Paton who sailed to Tanna in the New Hebrides and built a house in Port Resolution with the intention of converting indigenous inhabitants from cannibalism to Protestantism. Motivated by these findings I decided to have FOF's stories published and they lead the way for more family members' stories to be enjoyed.

# 1 ~ A HERO
## by
## Frederick Oscar Finlayson (1848 – 1944)

Did you ever hear of the wreck of the **Royal Charter**? No? Well, of course, it's a long time ago, but what happened was like this:

The **Royal Charter** was homeward bound from Australia with emigrants from Liverpool and she foundered when she ran aground off Anglesey in a terrible storm.

Well, in those days there was no rocket apparatus and such-like, and it was impossible to launch boats in such boiling seas among the rocks. It seemed as if all on board must be lost. But there was one man who said he would swim ashore with a line. In a boiling sea like that it was just like committing suicide, for it seemed he was certain to be dashed to pieces on the rocks. Anyway, he went, and lived to tell the tale! He got ashore with a line fastened to his body, and was the means of saving many lives. Oh yes, there was a great lot about it in the illustrated journals of the time, and a fine deed it was, and a great deal was made of it.

Some time after, when I was in Melbourne, we had been loading cargo brought by our ship from along the coast. The **British Queen** was lying at Melbourne. A great towering ship she was – miles above us in the dock – and in the evening we sailors often went aboard her, yarning with her crew. One evening I went aboard her and the talk got round to the wreck of the **Royal Charter** and what a fine deed that man did. I said that I would very much like to have met that man.

"Would you?" said one of the crew.

"Yes," said I, "that I would".

"Well," said he, "you shall. I can take you to him."

"Nonsense," said I. "It's not likely I should ever see him! What do you mean, you can take me to him?"

"Because," says he, "he's aboard this very ship."

"What?" says I. "You mean to tell me he's aboard the **British Queen**?"

"Yes," he says, "he is. Come along with me."

I followed after him, right down into the ship, and it was all dark and we could hardly see our way. Presently, somewhere nearby in the gloom, I could hear someone singing "Gard safe ah grachus Quin, larng lif ah nobel Quin." Directly I heard it, I knew this singer was a foreigner, and a man came along towards us.

"Here's so-and-so." (I forget his name now) said the sailor who was with me. "Show this fellow your medal, he'd like to see it."

The fellow opened his shirt and showed us a medal – and there it was – on one side there was a picture of the wreck and on the other side his name, and the date, and a few words about the circumstances. And that was the man who'd swum ashore with a line through the boiling sea and saved ever so many lives.

"Well," I said afterwards, "What is he? What does he do aboard this ship?"

"He's the lamp trimmer," said the sailor.

"The lamp trimmer?" says I. "The lamp trimmer? Why, a man like that ought to be riding about in a carriage, leading the life of a gentleman, without a care in the world. Do you mean to say that nothing was ever done for a man like that?"

"Well, you see," said the sailor, "he wouldn't take anything for what he'd done, no amount of money, or anything else. He wouldn't have a thing except that medal around his neck that he showed you. That was all he would accept. And here he is aboard this ship, and he calls himself the lamp trimmer. But, as a matter of fact, he does just about anything he likes – little or much – and that's what he's called – the lamp trimmer."

Now, wasn't he a brave man to do such an heroic thing?

# 2 ~ ABOARD THE RUSSELL CASTLE

There was one ship everybody wanted to sail in. There was a saying amongst the sailors in Melbourne at the time, that the only chance to get aboard that ship was if you saw a coffin being carried ashore. The ship was the ***Russell Castle*** skippered by Captain MacIntosh.

Well, I got on that ship, and this is how it happened.

I was lodging with a policeman at the time, between voyages and one night I had just gone upstairs and was preparing to go to bed – quite late – when there was a knock on the door. My bedroom door was still open and when the policeman went to the door I heard a man say:

"Does Fred Finlayson live here?"

"Yes," says the policeman, "he's here."

"Well," says the man,

"I'm the carpenter from the ***Russell Castle***. She's sailing in the morning and one of the men is ill and can't sail; and the Captain will want another man, but he'll have to come at once and go on board tonight. I thought it very likely that Fred would like to go."

Well, as soon as I'd heard my name, I'd pricked up my ears, and long before the carpenter had said all that, I'd started to collect my things together into a bag, and in a very short time I was ready. I said goodbye to the policeman and his wife and away we went, down to the docks, and rowed out to the ship. Later, when the Captain came aboard, I was signed on, And there I was, aboard the ***Russell Castle***!

Now I'd heard a lot about that ship – what a grand life it was, and how well the men were looked after – but I didn't expect to see what I did see! You know, in those days sailors were not looked after like they are now, but on this ship there were pens with pigs, sheep and chickens in them; plenty of fruit for everybody; and the Captain was a very nice man. He took great care of his ship and everyone in it.

I was talking to him about it all one day – the pigs and all that – and he said:

"Well you know, Fred, I am thinking about myself as much as you – having all this fresh meat handy – and so on. The way I look at it is, if I look after you all well, I get good work, so you see it's not all you and nothing else I'm thinking of."

He was a very nice man, the Captain.

Well, on such a good ship, and so difficult to get on board her, you'll be wondering why I left her. The reason was a mate we had. Oh, an awful man. How he ever got his ticket I don't know! He knew no more about the job of First Mate than you do! Not even half as much! He was a regular bully. He used to abuse the men and make their lives a misery, and all the time most of us knew a great deal more about sailoring than he did.

One time when we were nearing port, and I thought I couldn't stand the bully any longer, I told the Captain I wouldn't ship again on the next voyage. He asked me the reason, and I told him. He talked to me and reasoned about it.

"Here you are," he said, "on a well-found ship, and just because of that one man, you're going to throw away the chance of staying on her for goodness knows how long. Why don't you try to put up with it? You know, Fred," he said, "it might not be for long."

I ought to have weighed his words, which were as much as he could say to me about an officer; but I was young then, and headstrong, and I wouldn't listen, and when we reached port I was paid off and left that ship for good. The chance of re-joining her never came my way again.

Afterwards, I heard what was the end of that mate. The Captain was right. If I'd put up with him and stayed on the ship, it wouldn't have been for much longer.

I forget whether it was the very next voyage, but anyway, it wasn't very long afterwards. The ship went round from Melbourne to Newcastle in Australia, and was going to ship a new mast there. Every morning the Captain went ashore to the offices on business, and left the Mate in charge to see to the work of the ship, and in particular, to the job of the mast. The Captain would be gone for most of the day. Well, that Mate knew absolutely nothing whatever about the job of the mast, and as soon as the Captain had been gone a short while, off he went too; and left the hands to attend to the mast – and for that matter they knew a great deal more about it than he did – and he would come back again a little time before the Captain usually returned. This went on for some days.

Then, one morning, the Captain went ashore as usual and, also as usual soon after, the Mate went ashore. However, after about an hour, the Captain came back. He had a look at the new mast and asked where the Mate was. He was told he'd gone ashore. The Captain asked a lot more questions and heard about the Mate going ashore every day. Maybe the Captain knew, or guessed something of it already, and that's why he'd come back unexpectedly. I don't know. The men didn't hear anything more about it, but the Mate went at the end of that voyage.

It's a mystery to me to this day, how that man ever got his Mate's ticket.

# 3 ~ SURPRISES ALL ROUND

This happened when I was aboard the Missionary Ship ***Dayspring*** – sister ship to the ***John Williams*** – cruising about the New Hebrides. Mr. English, the Missionary, and his wife were on the ship.

We also had some half-a-dozen young Missionaries and their wives on the ship, going to the different stations. It was a beautiful day – such a warm balmy climate it was, and everything so clear and pure – I can well understand the mutineers of the **"Bounty"** not wanting to come away from those latitudes. The ship was just slowly gliding along in the water. She was nearly all saloon and on the deck above, all those young ladies were sitting about dressed in their muslins and laces and so on, and very canny and bonny I must say they did look.

Well presently along comes all these canoes. The islanders knew this Missionary ship. She was all painted white – and they were that glad to see her. The Captain gave the word to throw ropes over the side and they all clambered up like a lot of brown monkeys – most hadn't waited for the ropes.

Those men were only one very small degree removed from beasts. I've had plenty of experience amongst Zulus and they, and the Basutos, and even the Kaffirs – all fine upstanding men – stand up straight and look you in the eye; but these locals – well they were more like monkeys – sharp, thin and lithe, quick as lightening in their movements, but running and tumbling along with knees bent, and prancing about just the same as monkeys do – never stood up straight!

Directly these fellows got on board – well, I shall never forget it! I laughed so much at those men. They rushed straight at those young ladies, feeling them all over, handling their laces and clothing, chattering and laughing, just the same as a lot of monkeys.

Well it was pretty plain to see that these young ladies had not been prepared for what to expect. They were properly frightened and disgusted. The poor fellows didn't mean them any harm, of course, but the young ladies were quite taken by surprise. They tried to get down below, but Mr. English wouldn't let them. "No", he said. He reminded them that they had come out there to rectify that sort of thing, and they must not let the poor fellows see how they felt. No harm was intended! He wouldn't let them go below.

We had on that ship a black cook. Black as coal he was – an African of some sort – educated and all that, but black as coal. He was an enormous fat man. One of the Islanders caught sight of the cook staring open-mouthed at them, and he shouted something to the others, and they all made a great rush at the cook. He snatched up a great cook's knife and flourished it at them.

"Come on, you black buggers," he roars.

Of course they stopped – they're soon terrified. Oh dear, how I had to laugh at that cook! There he was, on a *religious* ship, where prayers are said every day, flourishing a great sharp knife and yelling "Come on you black buggers!" Well, they thought he must be a devil or something of the kind, and they all tumbled over the side helter-skelter into the sea, and swam for their canoes. They all swam like fishes! They weren't waiting for the help of any ropes to get down – away they went – head-first over the side. How I did laugh.

But they weren't going to hurt the cook – they only wanted to feel him to find out whether he was real or not.

# 4 ~ THE ISLAND OF MALAKULA

One day when I was on the Missionary ship ***Dayspring***, it was a dead calm sea, overpoweringly hot, not a breath of air. I was standing holding the wheel, smoking and thinking. Presently the Captain came up in his white trousers and coat, and a cigar in his mouth. He stood a moment or two, had a look at the binnacle, and then stood looking ahead underneath the boom.

Suddenly he said sharply "Put the wheel down – put it down – that's it – right down." I put it down as he instructed.

Well, you know, in those latitudes it sometimes happens that a hurricane comes up all of a sudden, no matter how calm it is, and not a cloud to be seen. I said:

"What's the matter Captain? Expecting a hurricane?"

"No," he says, then pointing under the boom – "Look yonder – right over there – can you see anything?"

I looked. After straining my eyes a bit I could just make out a dark line.

"Yes," I says; "I do see something. It looks like land – rather like a chimney – you might almost think smoke was coming out of it," but the heat haze and the distance made it indistinct.

"It is land," says the Captain. "What you see is the smoke from a volcano. That is the island of Malakula. They're all cannibals there. We don't want them to see us."

"Well, what if they are?" says I, "they can't hurt us." (You see I was very green in those days).

"Oh, can't they?" says he. "Well, although they're cannibals, they're wise enough to know that in a calm like this we can't get away from them. They've any amount of canoes – once they spot us they'll be away in their canoes and surround us. With their bows and arrows they'll have us at their mercy. We're a peaceful Missionary sailing ship – unarmed."

By this time the ship was slowly coming round with her stern to the island.

"Well, Fred," said the Captain. "We can't get steerage on her, but keep her round like that; we must get away out of sight as soon as we can. We must have drifted further than I thought. I never meant to come within sight of that island."

So there we were, almost on top of the island of Malakula, but fortunately we got away without the islanders seeing us.

# 5 ~ HAPPENINGS IN TANNA

The island of Tanna is – or was in those far-off days – in three divisions, and the natives of one division were hostile to the others. In one of these divisions the natives were cannibals, and we couldn't land there. If one happened to get near the boundary of that division, the natives would kill and eat people.

There is a little port – Port Resolution – in the island. The entrance opens out of a round bay. Dr. Paton, the Missionary, lived there.

Well, these cannibals had been having a grand rumpus, and Dr. Paton was getting anxious, as they were getting very war-like and hostile. He got word sent away to the mainland (Australia) about the disturbance, and that he wanted help.

Orders were sent to a man-o'-war cruising about those different stations; the man-o'-war was the "**Rosario**". She got orders to go down to Tanna and do all she could to frighten the natives – fire some shots over the island – rockets and things – everything and anything they could to quieten them – but not to kill anybody.

So the **Rosario** came opposite to Port Resolution where Dr. Paton lived, and fired some shells. Those shells exploded in the air, and so they got to know all over the island about this man-o'-war, and islanders came running down to the beach with their clubs, and bows and arrows, and spears, from all quarters, to fight the man-o'-war.

Well, there was a batch of them coming through the bush – rushing along with their spiked clubs and whatnots – I can just fancy I see the beggars running with their clubs and things to fight the man-o'-war. There was a wide open space of ground, and when they came to this place they saw something lying on the ground. It was a live, unexploded shell. They didn't know what to make of it, and what it might be.

After they had had a bit of a palaver and consultation amongst themselves, they started hammering and banging it with their knobbly sticks and spears. Of course, it exploded and blew most of them to smithereens.

Yes – I can fancy I see the beggars coming up and wondering what it was, and then starting to bang the thing to bits! Some of the natives that survived told the Missionary later, what had happened, and that's how I heard about it.

# 6 ~ THE FIRST WHITE MAN

There was a very old man, an Islander, I couldn't say how old he was. He just had a few little bits of white fluff left on his head. An apprentice that we had on board, who understood their language a bit, interpreted for us what this old man said.

The old chap came aboard one evening, and we were asking him if he could recollect the first white man he'd ever seen, and what he thought of him.

I'll give you as near as I can to what he said – that is – as the interpreter told us:

It was blowing a gale and a ship in distress was drifting onto the island. There was a big coral reef there forming a harbour, and there was an opening in the coral reef where the ship could have come through (the same as we did). The coral reef acted as a breakwater. Well, the ship was drifting on to this coral reef and instead of coming through the opening she came right onto the reef. Then she broke up. The sea smashed her to bits. All the driftwood was floating about. Presently, the locals that were watching (including this old man, only he was a young man then), saw something white upon a bit of timber. It came through the opening onto the beach where the locals were standing. It was a white man!

Well, they got hold of him, and didn't know what to make of him. He was crying out to them not to hurt him, and getting on his knees begging them to spare his life. But they couldn't understand what he said. They decided they would tie his legs and arms for fear he did them any harm. They didn't know whether he was a devil or not!

It's a funny thing about all those natives – they have great notions about a devil – but no notions about God!

After they had tied his legs and arms they had a grand consultation as to what they were to do with him. At last it was decided that they should take a bit of flint stone and cut him. If blood came out of the cut he was human like themselves. If no blood came out, he must be a devil or a spirit of some kind. So they took a sharp stone and cut him and, of course, blood came out.

Then they had a grand dance of jollification because they were cannibals and he was meat for them. They made some fires and took a sharp stone (because they had nothing but flints to use in those days). They cut a lump of flesh off the man and put it on the hot stones over the fire and frizzled it. When it was cooked they cut it into pieces and handed it around to eat amongst themselves. Then they cut another lump off and roasted that in the same way, and again divided it amongst themselves. All the time the white chap was screaming with agony of pain and begging and entreating them to stop.

It would make your heart bleed to hear it the way that old chap was telling it. One of the crew asked if they had no notion that they were killing the man.

"No," he said.

They had no idea that they were killing him. They just kept cutting off pieces of flesh, roasting and eating it, until the poor fellow succumbed to death with agony, loss of blood and sheer terror.

There now – wasn't that an awful affair? It sickens you just to think of it. Eh?

# 7 ~ A LEAP IN THE DARK

This story happened during a voyage home, after we'd unloaded coal at Panama, and were lying off waiting to proceed to the Chinchas. We were near some small island, where we had unloaded the coal into hulks there for the purpose, and these islands were inhabited by a rare crowd of doubtful-looking Spaniards – a nasty lot, most of them, and I didn't care for the look of them at all. Far away in the distance we could only just see Panama itself.

Leaning over the side, I could see far down into the depths, and it must be seen to be believed, the crowd of life there is in those waters! They were thick with sharks, amongst other things, scores of them!

We were in a British ship, on account of wanting to get home from Australia, and in those days the British ships were awful – and this one was no exception. Those of us who had been used to the Australian ships felt it badly, and took up very badly indeed with the conditions. The Captain was all right, but the grub was awful, although this ship was no worse than other Britishers at the time.

Well, me and another chap had been talking all the way up to Panama about it and decided we would leave the ship as soon as we got a chance. The only thing that I wanted was to get home, and it might as well be one British ship as another! However, while we were lying off Panama, this fellow said we could swim ashore in the night to the islands and get away.

"Well," I said, "I would be very glad to leave the ship, but I value my life." I wanted to get home and I had no intention of jumping into those shark-infested waters.

You see, even if I did succeed in swimming the long distance to shore safely, which seemed most improbable, I didn't fancy landing among the people who inhabited those islands. If I escaped the sharks it seemed more than likely that I would come to grief at the hands of the inhabitants. However, he was determined that he would try and what's more, he would try that very night.

During the darkest and quietest part of the night he came up to me where I was standing leaning on the rail, smoking my pipe, and looking out into the darkness. He had his belongings in a bundle, strapped on his shoulders high up. After saying "Goodbye" and "Good Luck" he slipped quietly over the side and into the sea.

For a long time I watched the bundle getting further and further away from the ship, until at last I could see no more in the darkness.

For a long time I waited there, leaning on the rail, listening, thinking all the time that I would hear his screams as a shark got him; but I heard no sound, and I stood there a very long time – far longer than it would have taken him to reach the land. I've often thought about that sailor and wondered whether he got across safely. Thinking about that vast crowd of sharks, it doesn't seem possible.

# 8 ~ PIGS AT SEA

When sailing ships were going around the South Sea Islands, if there were any natives that would like to go to another island to see the people there, we took them. There was a special place up in the fore-part of the ship with bunks 'n' all, for the likes of them people. Sometimes we took five or six of them at a time, then we would collect them on our way back and land them on their own island again or, if another ship passed sooner, that vessel would take them home. Generally these islanders took a lot of presents with them for the people they were going to visit.

On this particular night, we had six of these natives on board and they each took a pig with them for presents. The pigs were put in the bow of the ship. Most of the ships have pig sties on board you know, to keep pigs in as food for the crew.

Well, on the third night of the voyage it came on to blow a regular hurricane. The wind was howling; the ship was pitching and tossing, and great waves were breaking over the bow of the ship. Every time the water came over, it touched the pigs, and they squealed and shrieked out.

These natives had never been afloat in anything the of the like of this storm before, and the poor beggars were frightened to death. Terrified, they came to see if they could sleep with us sailors in our quarters. But we didn't want them, so there they were, on their hands and knees, wailing and pleading with us to let them stay with us, where they felt they would be safer.

Well, we had an apprentice on board that ship who had been to that group of islands a couple of years before, and he'd got to understand their language a little bit. He told us that they were saying that if we would let them go into our quarters they would sleep on the floor under our bunks, right out of our way, just like dogs.

In the end we took pity on them and let them come in. They crawled into any dark corner they could find and curled themselves up so that they wouldn't bother us. They were very truly grateful.

Later that night when it was very dark, and the hurricane was still blowing, they had come out of their hiding places and were grouped closely together on their knees, muttering. We could hear them, but we didn't know what they were saying. Suddenly our apprentice burst out laughing.

"What's the matter?" we asked. "What are you laughing at?"

"They're praying," he says. "But you'll never guess what they're praying for!"

"Oh?" Says us. "What are they praying for?"

"They're praying that God will save their pigs. Not one of them has prayed for God to stop the storm – or save themselves, or us, – or our ship. They're only praying for Him to save their pigs."

I'll never forget that night – the ship tossing; the hurricane blowing; and every time the sea that came over the bow of the ship making the pigs squeal out – there's no wonder that those poor natives were on their knees praying. But you'd think they'd be praying for God to save their lives, not their blooming pigs!

# 9 ~ WHEN I CAME HOME IN 1870

I well remember the experiences we had on the ship in which I came home in 1870.

We had loaded coal at Newcastle, Australia, for Panama. After we had been there we came down the coast of Peru to the Chinchas Islands where we loaded guano for Mauritius. Oh, what terrible stuff that was to load! Most of the men were nigh suffocated with the stuff and every now and then hung over the sides of the boats for a bit, with their faces as close as they could get to the water to get a bit of breath.

After that we sailed on – down to the coast of Chile, round the Horn – and a good passage round we had too – and then East in a straight line for the Cape of Good Hope and Mauritius.

That was an awful passage, amongst great big icebergs and great fields of ice, and a great gale of wind blowing nearly all the time.

Well, after passing the Horn, while we were sailing across those cold Antarctic seas, we passed by miles and miles of ice-fields and saw gigantic icebergs, like great cities they were. I can't hardly describe them – sometimes shining in the sun, all beautiful colours with spires and turrets and great domes; like, maybe, St. Paul's Cathedral. Wonderful! I shall never forget the wonderful sights we saw then.

One night – it was my watch below – we were all roused by the shout of "All hands on deck!" Of course we knew something serious was on. We could hear the chains rattling, and no end of a noise of shouting orders and so forth as we tumbled out and up on deck, and my word, what a fright I got! My heart seemed to come into my mouth. I expect a good many more felt the same. Towering right above us – so close you could have thrown a biscuit onto it – there was a huge iceberg. The ship was so close, it seemed she must have struck it; and there it towered high above us in the darkness, shining with a horrible livid blueness. So sudden it was, and so overpoweringly close, I was mortally horrified by the sight of the awful thing. The ship was slowly manoeuvred about and by a miracle, cleared it.

I've always been given to understand that there is no hope for a ship that gets near a big iceberg on account of there being a certain amount of suction, however, we could not have been any nearer without having actually struck, yet we cleared it somehow.

Afterwards we found that what had happened was this: The Captain had come up on deck and stood near the steersman at the wheel. The boom and the sail hid the great iceberg from the view of the steersman and from the Captain too, as he stood next to him. The Captain, however, happened to stoop down and peer under the boom – and just in the nick of time he saw that the ship was heading right into the iceberg. He immediately shouted orders, and all that was possible was done. Fortunately we were able to clear the 'berg.

The look-out man – a foreigner – who should have been keeping a keen eye open for such things was found tucked away out of the wind and bitter cold, asleep with his coat muffled over his head. But for the Captain coming out on deck just when he did, we should have all been lost.

A further experience on that journey was when we were about half-way between the two Capes. A great big wave rolled up alongside and broke (or curled) right on top of us, carrying away all our bulwarks on both sides. Our decks were swept! At the same time our big main topsail yard snapped in two. Half of the yard was fast aloft, and the other half was hanging by some of the bolt ropes and swinging backwards and forwards right across the deck every roll the ship gave. How it was that none of us were killed or washed overboard I don't know. Of course, we had to man the pumps, and they had to be kept going many days until we got into smoother water. That was an awful time, keeping the pumps going with sea washing over us in such freezing weather. We had to be lashed to the pumps. I never thought we would have lived through it, but we got to Mauritius, and had to go into dry dock to have new bulwarks. When that, and other repairs were done, we loaded sugar for an order in Queenstown in Ireland and set sail for the Cape of Good Hope, and home.

The worst item between there and Ireland was when about half way up the Atlantic, in the Tropics, when we were going about with bare legs and feet. Some careless person had shoved the grainse beneath an upturned boat on the poop deck and never made it fast, so that one dark night this grainse had rolled from under the boat. The mate came running along and sent his foot with force against the prongs of the grainse. Three prongs went right into his foot.

I don't know if you know what the grainse is – it's like Neptune's trident, with barbs on the end of each prong, and it's used to spear fish with. It has a long shank – much larger than a broom shank.

Well, they had to get this poor man and the grainse under the cabin skylight, and get all the lamps they could, and the Captain had to take a lance and cut the barbs out of his foot. Rather a delicate job, eh? I was glad that I was in the bows of the ship on the "look-out", so I didn't see the process, but I could hear the poor chap crying out.

On another occasion, we had a cold and rough time crossing the Bay of Biscay, but it was much worse when we got to the Irish Sea in about the middle of January. It was blowing a regular hurricane right in our teeth so that we were close hauled under close reefed topsails on a lee shore, which means that we were drifting more sideways onto the shore than we were going ahead. It was awfully cold, with rain, sleet and snow. The last day out things were getting very serious. All day we were watching the surf breaking on the rocks at Queenstown Harbour and we were expecting to get landed on top of them before we could open out, but we did miss them, though it was a narrow squeak. About twelve o'clock that night came the cry "Hard up! Square the yards! Clew up. Stow the topsails." Oh, what a relief that was! The yards were soon squared; and as the topsails were already close reefed, it didn't take long to stow them; and there we were, running like a racehorse before the gale, straight into Queenstown Harbour, under bare poles.

There were a good many lights of ships at anchor in the harbour. It was very dark, and on account of the sleet and snow we couldn't see very far. Most of us chaps were down on deck standing by the cable chain, ready to pay it out when the anchor was let go. As our bulwarks were very high we couldn't see over them. Soon the cry came "Let go!" The anchor was let go. At the same instant there was a terrible crash and the big ship trembled from stem to stern.

"What the hell is the matter now?" we heard a voice say, and we all skedaddled up onto the foc'sale deck, to find that we had run right onto a French schooner. We'd dropped our anchor onto his decks and cut him down to the water edge. Our jib-boom and bowsprit was sticking right over the top of him.

The reason we hadn't seen him was because all the Frenchies were asleep in their bunks, and there were NO LIGHTS UP IN THE RIGGING. The crash sent all the Frenchies scrambling on deck, thinking they'd been done for. It would've made you laugh if you'd heard the blessings that our men hurled on them! We'd been thinking that as soon as the anchor was let go, it would be off oilskins and sea-boots, etc. and into the bunks between the blankets, whereas now there was a long job in front of us. We had to set-to and cut ourselves clear of the other ship; run a small anchor some distance away; haul ourselves clear; and drop our anchor in another place. When all that was done it was breakfast time, and we were ready for it, I can tell you! After breakfast we got rolled up in the blankets and slept there all day.

We were laid in Queenstown harbour for about three weeks, then we got our orders for Bristol. There was not much wind coming across to England but it was blowing a gale coming up the Bristol Channel on a Saturday night. We dropped anchor at the mouth of the river and lay there till the Monday morning, when a tug-boat came and towed us up to Bristol Docks.

So ended the worst voyage I've ever had.

# DEAR DOMINIC

## BY

## MARGARET COX

Margaret Cox (née Kilcullen) aged about 21

# INTRODUCTION

Margaret Cox (née Kilcullen) was one of my mother's cousins. Although I never knew Margaret personally, she was a very good friend of my mother's younger sister, Doris Watson, née Pritchard, and I heard a lot about her from my Aunt.

Margaret's son, John Cox, through another of my mother's cousins, Mike Race, very kindly loaned me a copy of a letter which Margaret started to write when she was 83 years of age and finished when she was 86. Her tenacity to complete her autobiography is commendable. It reflects the Pritchard spirit of determination to achieve well. Margaret's ambition to turn the clock back for her family's enlightenment of her life-time experiences came to an end when she finally put a kiss on the paper and put her pen down in 1984. Unfortunately she will never know that the desire she expressed in the first line of her story, to become a published writer, has come true; but her family will know and no doubt continue to be very proud of her.

I thought it was a remarkable achievement to be able to remember facts accurately and write them down so clearly. I was enthralled by her story. It inspired me to start writing as a pastime in the leisure hours of my retirement. I felt if Margaret could write like this, in her eighties, why was I holding back when I was a quarter of a century younger? I joined a creative writing group, had short stories published in books and magazines, and produced a début novel, all as a result of reading her letter.

Over a decade later I was very kindly given permission to include Margaret's life story in a book of memoirs by some Pritchard family members. I hope you will enjoy reading it as much as I did.

# DEAR DOMINIC
## by
## Margaret Cox (1898 – 1987)

### 19TH MARCH 1981

Dear Dominic,

Throughout my life I have felt the urge to write a book but never made the attempt because I thought I would not be competent enough to do it. I am sitting in my sitting room at No 7 Rydal Avenue, York, when I thought to myself: "Why don't I write a story for my beloved Grandson, Dominic?" This story is a true story about myself. It may sound very egotistical and it is. Your grandfather, Jack Cox, always said I was "a big head" and he was right.

Like all stories, I will start at the beginning.

I was born on 7th October 1898 at 25 Spencer Street, Nunnery Lane, York, the only child of Edward William Kilcullen and Margaret Kilcullen (née Pritchard).

My father was a masseur at the Turkish Baths in St Sampson's Square. W P Brown Ltd has a shop there now on the site. I did not stay very long at Spencer Street because I remember having my fourth birthday at 11 Little Stonegate where my maternal grandmother lived in a very big house at the corner of Swinegate and Little Stonegate. It was joined by another house, and one could walk from one house to another without going outside.

The houses were previously rented by a doctor who must have had a staff of servants because there were bells on the wall of the kitchen. Underneath each bell there was a number, which showed the servants which room to go to. I was fascinated by this. Of course my grandmother did not have servants (except my mother who worked like a slave for no money). She – grandma – had "lodgers" – in present day language "paying guests". My mother was married from that house on 2nd August 1897 at St Wilfrid's Church, York. (Dad died on 1st August 1932. (His 62nd birthday).

Shortly after my fourth birthday we went to live in Bradford. My father was born in Bradford in 1870. Mother did not like living in Bradford so we came back to York when I was seven years old and again we went to live with grandma. This time she had not such a grand house and once again she had "two houses", this time in the Shambles, where at that time there were quite a number of butchers.

The "front house" was where I lived and grandma ran a second-hand clothes shop, a very profitable business at that time. The second house had to be approached from the street and up a passage at the side of the "front" house. Some other members of the family lived in that house which at one time had been a public house. Its name was "The Shoulder of Mutton".

At the time that I lived in the Shambles there were two public houses, one was called "The Eagle and Child", the landlord at one time being a Mr Waddington. The other was at the bottom of the Shambles. (Dewhurst butchers were there on that site and probably are now). It was called "The Globe". The landlord there was a Mr Stephenson, and when he died his widow took over the licence. They had two sons and one daughter called Emily, with whom I used to play, and was always invited to her parties.

A few of the girls of my age who lived in the neighbourhood were "stage struck" and we used to dress up in long dresses and fancy hats and pretended we were on the stage. Apart from myself there were Emily Stephenson, Annie Robinson whose parents had "The Blue Bell" in Fossgate, and Amy Stott. Annie Robinson's sister, Edith Pinder, is still the landlady of the "Blue Bell", it has been in their family for years – 70 to my knowledge. Amy Stott married a Mr Sutcliffe and her daughter-in-law was a member of the "York Amateurs" and your Nana knew her.

I must digress here and tell you that I was not the only member of my family who wanted to go on the stage. Three of them did. They were "first" cousins. "Tootsie" and Margaret Race went on the vaudeville stage. They did a song and dance routine and were called "The Sisters Race" but they did not like the life, touring from one town to another, so came home. The other relative was a "second cousin", Freda Gretton. She was a ballet dancer and moved in more exalted circles. Her grandmother, Emma Gretton, my mother's eldest sister, had somehow managed to arrange for Freda to stay with Sir Seymour Hicks and his wife Ellaline Terriss. Her stage career did not last either and she came home and married her Solly Morris and they had two children Philip and Annette. Unfortunately she died at an early age (22, I think).

I think I was about nine or ten when we moved house again, this time to another big house, No 4 King's Square. Immediately before grandma rented it, it was a public house called "Ye Olde Turk's Head". There were six bedrooms and a lavatory upstairs but no bathroom, five rooms downstairs, one of which was converted into a shop – second-hand clothes again. How I hated that shop!

On each side of the house was a butcher's shop. A Mr Linfoot and a Mr Ellis. Next door to Mr Ellis was a little public house, the name of which no one seemed to know because it was always referred to as "The Sawdust Hole". The landlord was Wallace Dawson who was a friend of your Great-grandfather and was a very good swimmer. There was a shield called "The York Shield" and the winner of the Yorkshire Swimming Championship held it for one year. Mr Dawson won this shield several times until 1897 when my father came to York. From then on it was marked Edward Kilcullen until 1914. I don't know what happened to that shield after that, but if you are sufficiently interested you could make enquiries from the York Swimming Association. Aren't you a lucky boy having *two* Great-grandfathers who were famous swimmers? Your mother's Grandfather, your Great-grandfather Carruthers, was also a famous footballer. Your Nana will show you the "Cup" he won.

I went to St Wilfrid's Roman Catholic School in Monkgate but to reach the school we had to walk up Lord Mayor's Walk and then down Groves Lane.

Incidentally, my mother was born at 19 Lord Mayor's Walk on 27th January 1875.

When we lived in Bradford I went to a private school called St Patrick's and the fee was six pence a week in old currency (2½p in present-day currency). I got a good start and I always liked studying (and still do – I went to night-school at the age of 79 to try and learn French but only managed one course).

When I was fourteen, the age of school leaving at that time, the Parish Priest of St Wilfrid's, a Provost Dawson, wanted to pay for my education in Belgium but my mother would not let me go. (By the look of my spelling mistakes I think I should go to night-school to learn to spell).

Unlike you, I did not have a happy childhood. I was not unhappy, but I would have preferred to live just with my parents and not the hustle of people coming in and out of the house all the time.

My mother's sister, Agnes Stabler, was the first landlady of the Coach and Horses in Nessgate and as soon as I left school, at mid-day I had to go to the Coach and Horses, carrying a jug, and I collected Quaker Oats for my grandma. These were made by a cousin, Margaret Race, who lived with Aunt Agnes. Auntie was too busy to cook because she had to work in the bar. I did not understand then, and still do not understand, why I had to go to an Aunt for Quaker Oats when my mother was an excellent cook and cooked every day for ten people: Grandma and her second husband, Mr William Yates, Dad, Mother, and myself, plus the dressmaker, Mrs Boocock, and a shoe repairer – called "Cobbler" in those days and three lodgers. Although my grandma was fairly well off I didn't have a penny to spend so I had to rely on my father for pocket money.

Near where I lived was a cinema called "The Victoria Hall" where children could go to watch the "silent" pictures of those days. The film stars were Mary Pickford, Charlie Chaplin, "Fatty" Arbuckle and many others who are remembered to this day. I badly wanted to go one day, and asked my grandma if she would give me two pence so I could go to the cinema. She was horrified.

"Two pence? Where would I get two pence? Get your coat on and you can come out with me."

We had not walked very far when she saw a man who worked for the Corporation, sweeping the streets. She said to me:

"Oh, look, there's poor Charlie Bastey, go and give him this two shilling piece and tell him your Grandma, Mrs Pritchard, has sent it to him."

You can imagine my feelings as I thought "she would not give me two pence and yet she will give the crossing sweeper two shillings," which was a lot of money in those days.

Although my Grandma was called Yates, because of her second marriage no-one called her by that name because her first husband's name was Joseph Pritchard and of course all her children were called Pritchard – eight girls and one boy – all in the hotel business, except my mother. Probably that is why she was the Cinderella of the family.

I think my beloved Dad must have been fed up because although my Dad could have got work in the West Riding as Bath's Manager, which he did before he came to York, including Cleckheaton and Kirkstall, my mother did not fancy going to the Bradford area again. As there were no jobs vacant in that area he had to find some other kind of work. There were no Social Services in those days so one had to work or starve.

One day when he was out walking he met a very old friend called John Dowling, who was feeling very happy because he had just got a contract to build a house for Sir Newbold Kay. (Your Nana and Grandad are friends of Sir Newbold's descendants). Mr Dowling offered my father a job but as my Dad had not a "trade" he had to prove he was a <u>good</u> labourer. He worked as a labourer until six weeks before he died, with the exception of four years in the Army in the First World War 1914 -1918.

He was not a "combatant" or fighting soldier because when he was 17 years of age he had his thumb and first finger of his left hand amputated by a circular saw. Dad always referred to himself as a "Jekyll and Hyde" because he worked on a building site through the day and spent some of his leisure time by night with his friend, Gerald Merriman, who was a Pawnbroker in Petergate. Dad, Mr Merriman and I would go to watch boxing matches in Museum Street. One of the top boxers in York was Frank Fowler, Helena Fowler's grandfather.

When I was sixteen I went to work at the Royal Army Pay Office as a clerk. The office was on Wiggington Road. I stayed there for four years and then was lucky enough to get a job in the Railway offices.

After four years at the Pay Office I gave in my notice and went to work in the railway offices, where I spent ten very happy years. I started work in the "Rates Revision" office, then I decided I wanted to learn shorthand and typing so I wrote to a man called Mr Prime and I had to go to his house in the evening because I worked through the day. Later Mr Prime rented offices in Blake Street and became very successful. His pupils went during the day and he had so many, he had to employ a teacher.

When I was qualified as a shorthand typist I was transferred to the Mineral Rates office to work for the Mineral Rates Officer a man called Bromley whom I did not like very much.

In May 1925 I went to Rome with two of my father's sisters, Aunt Delia who came to England on a visit from America (Philadelphia PA) and Aunt Ruth who lived in Bradford, as it was "Holy week".

One of the biggest thrills of my life was standing on the railway station at Rome singing the hymn "Faith of our Father's Holy Faith, we will be true to Thee until death", and later when I kissed the hand of His Holiness the Pope in the Vatican.

The Mass in St Peter's Church was to "Canonise" a French girl who became a nun. She died at the age of 24 but lived in the same period as your Great-grandmother (my mother), and there was a French girl called Bernadette Soubirous who lived in Lourdes in the South of France, who is "Saint Bernadette" and she lived in the same period as your Great-great Grandma but my Grandma would be quite young when St Bernadette died.

When Bernadette was about 15 years of age she had visions of Our Lady, the Mother of God and Our Lady told her that she had to scratch the ground at a certain place and water would appear. After several visions of Our Lady the villagers got curious and wondered what Bernadette was doing, going to certain places quite often. These were on the days Our Lady indicated a particular spot. One day quite a number of people saw Bernadette scratching the ground and wondered what she was up to. Of course they could not see Our Lady, only Bernadette. Our Lady told Bernadette to go to the Priest and tell him to build a Church on the spot where she had stood and she wanted people to walk in procession. Bernadette asked Our Lady her name and Our Lady replied "I am the Immaculate Conception". (This means that Our Lady was born without the stain of Original Sin on her soul, as in every other human being). In our case the Original Sin is washed away by Baptism and I will never forget the day you were Baptised, and you were given the lovely name of Dominic. Our Lady had appeared to St. Dominic and said she would like people to say their "Hail Mary's" counting the number of prayers while they held the beads. I have given your Grandad Cox's rosary to you and hope if you use it you will remember me in your prayers.

## FRIDAY 30TH APRIL 1982

You will never believe this, Dominic, but I started to write to you on 19th March 1981. The preceding pages were written within a couple of days of that time and I did not write any more until now.

The reason I am writing now, 10 am, is because it is expected that our Royal Navy is due to start a blockade of the Falkland Islands. I have had more than my fair share of wars, because I was born 7th October 1898 and therefore was living during the time of the Boer War in South Africa, then the "Great War" which started on 4th August 1914 and ended 11th November 1918. Then the second World War starting in 1939 (I think the date was 3rd September) and ended with V.E. Day, (Victory in Europe) 8th May 1945 and V.J. Day (Victory in Japan) came weeks later.

This week I have been watching a TV Series 'I remember Nelson'. Many years ago a play came to York Theatre Royal called "In Nelson's Days". One of the lines spoken in this play was "Kilcullen is dead". As you know, Kilcullen was my maiden name. The man in the play must have been very insignificant, as I have not heard his name since. (The actor's real name I mean, not the part he played).

# 1ST MAY 1982 (ST JOSEPH'S DAY)

Yesterday my hopes rose when I heard that the Argentineans were going to withdraw their troops from the Falkland Islands. Alas, that did not happen and the BBC interrupted David Jacob's programme to announce we had made an attack on the Belgrano. I am not going to say any more about the Falkland Islands as you will learn about it in history. Instead I will go to when I was young.

I had a very happy life when I was working in the railway offices and did quite a bit of travelling in Europe. I went to Paris, France, for a holiday. My week in Paris cost me £5. When in later years I told your Daddy this he would not believe me but I assure you, Dominic, it is quite true. I spent my money wisely. Because I worked for the railway, I had concessions in travelling fares. My travelling from York to Paris was 8/6d (eight shillings and six pence); and £3-3-0 (three pounds, three shillings) for a very good hotel called Hotel Belle Vue in Rue Turkyo (I think I've remembered the name, but am not sure).

Obviously with the money I had to spend I could not afford to go to ballets or theatres, but as I was in Paris on the 14th July, their Independence Day, a lot of the pleasure I had was free. No one went to bed, the streets were thronged with people and there were bands, and people were dancing. My girl friend, Millie Waterhouse, who also worked in the railway offices and I sat at tables on the pavement outside a café, drinking coffee at two pence per cup.

Good gracious! Here it is 21st June 1983, and I started this in 1981. I had better persevere or I will never finish it.

I had better keep on with my "railway" days, which were wonderful. Having "passes" I could travel a lot and also I was a good dancer, and a <u>moderate</u> tennis player. I never would have qualified for playing at Wimbledon! Incidentally it is the annual tennis tournament at this particular time and I am hoping to watch Jo Durie on television this afternoon, but there is some doubt at the moment as the Outside Broadcasting Camera men are on strike. I was very disappointed that they "blacked" Royal Ascot last week as I had looked forward to seeing our beloved Queen riding in her carriage on the Royal course. During Ascot week the Queen stays at Windsor Castle and I once had the pleasure of visiting the Castle (where your Grandad used to do sentry duty there when he was a Guardsman in the 2$^{nd}$ Battalion of Scots Guards).

In 1927 Mam, Dad and I went to live at 24 Falsgrave Crescent, Burton Stone Lane.

During 1920 to 1930 working in the railway offices I had a wonderfully happy time. In 1926 I was recommended for a post as personal clerk to the Advertising Manager of the London and North Eastern Railway which I was happy to accept and spent four happy years working for him. He was a wonderful boss.

In 1928 I went to a dance at the Assembly Rooms and met your grandfather. He asked me to dance and I accepted. He was a marvellous dancer and I enjoyed dancing with him.

One of my friends at the dance told me he was a policeman and after that I saw him on "point" duty but we did not speak to each other. I was not particularly interested in him because at that time I was being courted by a young man called Jerry Markham who lived at 28 Brougham Street, Burnley, Lancs, and he used to come to York to see me and I would go to Burnley to see him. However, the romance came to an end when he ran over a child and he, the boy, was killed. Although it was not Jerry's fault (the child had run into the road without warning) he was in a dreadful state. He did not come to see me in York and did not suggest I should go to Burnley. I wrote him a letter and suggested he should emigrate. He did emigrate to America but had not the courtesy to write and tell me.

Years later his sister, her two children as I know them now, adults, came to York on an outing from Burnley and I saw her. She told me Jerry had gone to America, had married but had no children. He had brought his wife to England to meet his family.

Winnie (Jerry's sister) told me that right to her mother's dying day she had said:

"Our Jerry went further but foxed us. He should have married that lass from York."

This knowledge helped me to restore my pride. I had not liked being jilted. (I told you I was a big head).

However, to come back to 1928, I again met your grandfather and he asked if he could take me to the "pictures" (Cinema). From then on we went out together regularly and we were married on 28th June 1930. We had a big wedding. I was wearing a lovely white dress and orange blossom and veil. My bridesmaids were your great Aunt Eileen and my cousin, Janet Dobson. The reception was in the De Grey Rooms near the theatre and there were about 75 guests. We went to Douglas, Isle of Man. We were married at St Wilfrid's Church in Duncombe Place.

After our marriage I found I had a lot of time on my hands. As my mother was such a worker, she liked to do the housework. However, I regret to tell you I was happy about this as I am naturally a lazy person, domestically, but a workaholic when it was office work. I had to do some kind of work though, but as Police Regulations did not permit policemen's wives to go out to work I had to do voluntary work.

Great-grandad Cox and a few of his friends decided to form themselves into an organisation to help the York County Hospital, then in Monkgate, and called themselves "Ebor Hospital Workers". No National Health Service in those days, it was run by voluntary subscriptions. One or two women were in the group, including me, and I was voted to be the secretary. Jack did the organising (a born organiser if ever there was one). One of the events he organised was a fashion parade and cabaret. The lady who provided the dresses for modelling was a Mrs Foulds, neé Hawksby, and she had a shop in Stonegate and traded under the name of "Ernestina." It was great publicity for her. The audience had to choose some of the best outfits and the lucky ones were given prizes.

During that week there was performing in York at the Empire a well known vaudeville artist called Florrie Ford. She was an Australian lady and was famous for singing the old song "Down at the old Bull and Bush." She was a very tall lady and well proportioned. Jack asked her to present the prizes and she agreed. This event was held in the Rialto, Fishergate (later burnt down) and Jack Prendergast was the owner. He invited us to his room above the dance hall and we were eating and drinking until the early hours of the morning. You may be interested to know that Mr Prendergast's son was John Barry Prendergast (John Barry) the music composer.

Jack was made a Governor of the hospital for his good work.

In April 1932 we moved from Falsgrave Crescent to 18 Lucas Avenue, a Council property. It was a three bedroom house, with sitting room, dining room, and large garden. The rent was fifteen shillings and two pence per week. On 1st August 1932 my beloved father died of cancer of the liver. It was his 62nd birthday. The doctor at the hospital had told my mother that some doctors wept because they could not cure him. Apart from the cancer he was an extremely healthy man and could have lived until he was 90.

## 5TH OCTOBER 1983

I am going to digress here, because today is your seventh birthday and in two days' time it will be my birthday, my 85th. I just can't believe it because my mind, hearing and sight – also memory – are excellent. My physical trouble is I have arthritic knees which prevent me from being mobile. However, I accept the Will of God and thank him, inter alia, for the many blessings I have received; among them my beautiful grandchildren. I wish you and Francesca a long and happy life. If you are good you will not have many troubles, it is the bad things we do that causes misery.

In 1932 my father became ill. He would not stop work even though he was ill.

Your Grandpa Cox got the chance of a corporation house at 18 Lucas Avenue, not far from where we lived. It was a very nice house with a lovely garden, but the best thing about it was that it had a bathroom.

When I suggested to mother and father that we should all move to the new house Dad was a bit hesitant at first. He said to me:

"Do you realise what you are asking me to do? You are asking me to transfer my home to Jack." (The house had to be in Jack's name).

I said I had not realised that, and told him so. I said of course we would not move, but Dad said that Jack was an honourable man and would not do anything that was not right in that respect. He was right. We moved in April 1932 and he died on 1$^{st}$ August. His last words were "Jack – Mother" meaning Jack should look after mother. Mum and Jack lived together for 25 years and never once had a quarrel.

Things started to get bad money-wise shortly after Dad died. His wages had gone and Mother had a widow's pension which was ten shillings per week (Fifty pence in present day currency). Then Grandad Cox came home and said the Police had had their wages reduced by seven and sixpence per week and I said I would take that amount of money less in my housekeeping. However, some time after that there was another reduction of seven and sixpence per week which I could not reduce from the housekeeping. Grandad said he knew I could not and said he would take less "pocket money". Poor Dad. He just had a few shillings for himself. Luckily we each had a bicycle and would go for rides in the country and go swimming at Yearsley Baths.

I got friendly with my next-door-but-one neighbour whose husband worked at Rowntrees and they were on short time. She was a wonderful housekeeper and cook, and every Thursday we would go shopping together. We would go to the butchers and buy mince and breast of mutton, and ask the butcher to cut it in half. She would have the piece with the bones in and I would have the "thin" part and vice versa the following week. After shopping we went home and the baking started. (Not me, I was hopeless as a cook).

My neighbour, Mrs Quinn, had a beautiful little girl called Margaret (later she had one called Mary). Margaret adored Jack and he had bought her a little baking set. She would spend all day with us, but Thursday was her favourite day as it was baking day. Mother would give her a piece of pastry "dough" and she rolled out the same piece the whole of the day, and when it was nearly time for your Grandad to come home she asked my mother to put it in the oven to bake and proudly presented it to Jack and insisted on him eating it while she watched. It was black bright but he bravely ate it.

Jack was the first policeman in York to go on motor patrol. Previously they were on foot patrol. The turns were drastic. One turn was 8 am to 12 noon, then off duty until 3 pm and off again at 8 pm.

Monday was always washing day and my friend, Mrs Quinn, came in to see me and said:

"Hurry and get your washing done and then I will come round and have a cup of tea when Jack has gone back to work."

However on this particular day things did not work out as planned. At 12.15 pm your Grandad came home and said:

"Come on, love, lets go and have a swim at Yearsley Baths." I replied:

"Just give me five minutes to put the washing away."

Great-grandma Kilcullen would have the dinner ready when we returned. At 3 pm Mrs Quinn came and I was on my knees wiping the floor. She said:

"What have you been doing, you should have finished a long time ago." I said:

"Jack wanted me to go swimming so I went." She was horrified and said:

"Just imagine going swimming in the middle of washday." I said

"When my husband says "play" – I "play" – the work can wait for another time," and that was how it was for forty years.

In May 1934, Grandad Cox was ordered by the Chief Constable to live in a flat at the Fire Station. This was a blow to me but Grandad and Great-grandad were quite pleased because he would get seven and sixpence a week extra and mother liked it because she was a "townie" – having been brought up in a public house called the "Ship Inn" in Skeldergate, Cromwell Road – whereas I was a "country" woman.

Let me explain how Grandad Cox earned his extra seven and six pence.

In those days the Police did all the "Emergency" Services i.e. Fire Brigade work and Ambulance Service. If Grandad did police work from

6 am to 2 pm, unless there was a compliment of eight men, he could not leave the premises. I was hoping to go out in the afternoon but could not unless there were eight men on the night turn. Also if there was an accident through the night it was possible Jack would be called out.

One awful experience I had, Grandad and I were invited to a party at the Sergeants' Mess, Royal Army Medical Corps, Fulford Road. I did not drink alcohol at that time but Jack always liked his pint of beer (except in the days in 1902 when he could not afford it). After a very enjoyable evening we came home and although Jack was not drunk in the strict sense of the word, I would describe his condition as "merry". We had not been in bed long when there was a loud knock on the door. It was Police Constable Arthur Moore (later Inspector) who said Jack would have to take out the ambulance. Panic Stations! Was he in a fit condition to drive the ambulance? My mother came to the rescue. She brought a jar of pickled onions and made your unfortunate Grandfather drink the vinegar and we walked him up and down the living room and finally he went out. Good thing it was not an emergency. No one noticed he had had too much to drink and everything went off well. We laughed about it afterwards but it was frightening at the time.

Another thing – I did not like living in the Fire Station. We had to share lavatories and a bath. Sometimes I would go to have a bath only to find someone had been before and forgotten to clean it. Ugh! I had to clean the bath myself.

Another thing I did not like was that we wives took our turn at washing down the stone steps. I was unlucky in following Mrs Walker who was not the domesticated type. She would wash the steps with a mop and the job took her twenty minutes. The steps were no better after she had washed them. The following week I <u>scrubbed</u> the steps two at a time constantly changing the water with the result that it took the whole morning for me to do the job.

One day Mrs Parkin who had just moved into a flat "underneath the clock" came to see me and said that her neighbour had told her she must take her turn in washing the steps every other week. (There were only two flats "underneath the clock".) Mrs Parkin told me she had no intention of washing the steps as she was a GPO telephonist before she married. I said to her:

"Don't worry, I was the Personal Secretary to the Advertising Manager of the London and North Eastern Railway but that did not exempt me." Mrs Parkin washed the steps!

After living in Police Quarters we moved to 18 Lucas Avenue. (I have described life there previously).

In 1941 the Police removed the ban from policemen's wives working and I went to work at Headquarters Northern Command as a shorthand typist. The office at that time was at Ashfield House, Dringhouses. I bought a second-hand bicycle which was called a "sit up and beg." On the day I was due to start work I set off with my "bike" for Dringhouses. I carried my gas mask, which your grandfather had insisted on me taking. I was a laughing-stock, and refused to carry it after the first day.

The previous Sunday we took a ride to Dringhouses to see how long it would take me to get from Seventh Avenue to the office as we were not allowed much time for lunch. Your Daddy was two years old and rode on a little "saddle" on the bar of your Grandfather's bike. He (Daddy) seemed to enjoy it.

I started work on 18th June 1941 and finished (retired on 19th January 1969). After working in the typing "pool" for ten months the Senior Roman Catholic Chaplain, Northern Command, asked me if I would work for him. I declined as I said I had a two-year old son and did not want to work any extra hours than I was at present. He said if I would work for him he would promise I would not work any extra hours. Alas it did not happen that way.

Apart from the Chaplain being allowed a shorthand typist he also had a clerk who was a soldier. After two weeks of my working in the Chaplain's office the soldier was discharged on medical grounds. When I asked who was replacing him he said:

"No one, but you are an intelligent woman, you can cope."

Cope? It took me three months to realise how much clerical work was involved and as the Chaplain kept me fully occupied dictating letters there was not a hope of me doing the clerical work during office hours (we worked a minimum of 56 hours a week including half day on Sunday).

I decided I had better do some and go back in the evenings and work. One week I worked 75 hours and I did not get paid for the overtime. I can remember riding home on the old "sit up and beg" bike at 11 o'clock at night. (Your Nana will describe the bike to you, because although we had not met she used to see me riding my old bike). I bet I looked funny! When we were able to buy new bicycles I treated myself to a new Hercules bike. Low, and bright red with a basket on the front of the handle bars. I was certainly proud of that bike.

At this time your Grandad Cox was secretary of the Police Concert Party with marvellous entertainers. They were Topsy Biscomb, pianist, Inspector Charlie Barnard, baritone, Douglas Holder, tenor, Billy Bell, Ventriloquist and Bob Lawrence, conjurer. Betty Bell and her friend Monica, dancers, Ivy Wilson, singer and "Paddy" O'Gorman, Irish comedian, and of course your Grandad, top of the bill. They, the Concert Party, came under the jurisdiction of the Council for War Time Services and a special bus was provided to convey the artistes to various Army Camps to entertain the troops. One of the Camps was the airfield at Pocklington and I think your Daddy once went there with the York Police Concert party. The bus was an unusual one as there was a platform on which was a grand piano and the seats were in reverse order to a normal bus. This was in case they visited an ACK-ACK site where there were just a few men/women manning the guns. The man in charge of making the arrangements was Mr Kay, a Solicitor. * (I have forgotten his Christian name but your Nana will remember it. (Once again a member of the famous Kay family).

* I have just remembered his Christian name. A R T H U R.

Because of my working late hours it was often a case of "Hello Margaret – Goodbye Jack". If the party had to go a long distance it meant they had to have an early start.

My mother used to go to the Tang Hall Hotel to have her usual "Dutch Courage". She had only two drinks all the evening. She had a friend called Gertie O'Donnell and all the women customers used to sit in the hallway of the pub. The building has now been demolished and replaced with a monstrosity. The original building was owned by a woman called Starkey and she was reputed to carry a gun.

It did not occur to me to have a "baby sitter" for I would not leave your Daddy with anyone because of the possibility of air raids.

During the War the siren would warn us of approaching enemy planes and a different sound when it was "all clear". I would not bring your Daddy downstairs unless it was a long warning. We used to sit in a recess underneath the stairs. One night I brought your Daddy downstairs wrapped in a white shawl. I could hear bombs in the distance and was feeling a bit nervous. (Your Daddy would be four at this time and had just started St Aelred's School).

He went to school a few weeks before his fourth birthday (as my mother had fallen downstairs and was in hospital). I used to take your Daddy to school and he had to stay for his dinner and my friend, Mrs Wilkinson whose husband was a Police Sergeant went to school for him in the afternoon and he stayed with her until I came home from the office.

To go back to the bombing I started to sing a hymn called "Sweet Sacrament Divine" and I asked your Daddy what was his favourite hymn. He said: "Deep in the heart of Texas" – a song popular at that time.

He was not quite four at this period and had just started school due to the fact that my mother had fallen down the stairs and was in hospital. Her injuries were a dislocated shoulder and sprains. I had not drawn the curtains and as it was black-out time she was unable to put on the electric light and after being to the lavatory to return to her bedroom she missed her footing. An ambulance had to be called to take her to the hospital. Poor Mam! I told my "boss" Father Parisotti I would have to leave my job as I had an infant son to look after. He said

"You cant leave me in the middle of the war."

I told him my son was more important to me. That evening he came to the house with the Parish Priest, Father McAniff, and said he had given permission for your Daddy to go to school earlier than he should have done. The Headmistress was Miss Quirk who loved your Daddy very much. Every lunch time I would cycle to the school to see your Daddy. Mrs Wilkinson collected him in the afternoon. I often left the office early but he was quite happy staying with her as she had twin daughters, Hazel and Julia, a few years older than your Daddy.

One night I was feeling sorry for myself. I had started to do my weekly washing at 9 pm and was clearing up at 12 midnight. In my self-pity I started to cry and then a wave of our bombers flew over on their way to Germany. I said to myself:

"Why are you feeling sorry for yourself? Some of those airmen won't be coming back". I was right. We suffered heavy losses that night.

During the "Baedeker" (think I have spelt that word wrongly) on York, on 29th April 1942 your Grandad Cox was off work sick. When the siren went he got out of his bed to report for duty. I said to him:

"You don't have to report, because you are off sick," to which he replied:

"What kind of man do you think I am?"

I did not see him for three days. One of the police heroes at that time was PC Pybus but he did not get any recognition. Everyone was expected to do their duty.

Time went on with bombings, intermittently in York, but heavy in London, Coventry and Hull. The way of life for Londoners was to make their way to the Underground to spend the night making jokes and singing in the "Cockney" way.

Hull got a terrific amount of bombing but did not get as much publicity as London. In the early hours of one morning Grandad Cox came off duty. He had just returned from Hull. He said:

"Come and look through the back bedroom window."

There I saw a fierce blaze. I said:

"Is that Hull Road?" He said:

"No it is Hull."

Malta was heavily bombed and they never surrendered. They were very brave people and King George VI awarded the George Cross which was well deserved.

On 8th May 1945 came the Armistice and Germany surrendered. This date came to be known as "V E" Day – Victory in Europe. Sadly today people cannot remember the date. Enough of war which is now history.

In May 1950 your Daddy went to Boarding School at the Salesian College, Oxford. What an unhappy little boy he was and wrote letters asking to come home. Grandpa Cox said:

"Send for him to come home."

But I knew it would be a bad thing for him if he did. He came home every six weeks for a few days, so it was not too bad. Also there were several treats from the College like visits to other Salesian Colleges and Stratford-on-Avon.

All things come to an end and when your Daddy was sixteen he left the College for good. It was not until after you were born that your Daddy told me in your house that he was glad I had sent him to College and that made me feel much better. We were all happy to be together again.

In 1956 your Grandfather applied to go to Cyprus as a Sergeant Warder in the prison at Nicosia, where he had a miraculous escape from death.

My beloved mother seemed to wilt, after he had gone and kept saying:

"I wish I could see my 'son' just once." I said:

"He will be home next November and we will have a lovely party."

Alas, she died a few days before her 82nd birthday, but shortly before her death she received a letter from Grandad Cox enclosing £4 for a bottle of whisky and saying how much he loved her and how she had treated him better than his own mother had. I was glad she lived long enough to receive the letter.

Your Daddy was marvellous. He took over all the funeral arrangements and sent a cable to Cyprus to his father, who wanted to give up his job and come home, and I said "No".

Time goes on and in November 1957 he had earned quite a good bit of money and I had not spent the allowance he made me, living on my wages, so we bought a brand new Ford Anglia. We did not have it more than a few weeks and changed to a Consul. I will always remember the number ODN 777.

Before our marriage Grandad Cox had taken out an insurance policy for £200 and profit, for a period of 25 years. There were times when I found it difficult to find the sum of £2-3-4d each quarter and was annoyed that Grandad had taken out the policy without consulting me. Came the day it was due, I said:

"It has taken me twenty-five years to save this money and I am going to spend it on a holiday."

We chose to go to Spain and I thought we would settle at Sitges, 23 miles the other side of Barcelona. Grandad Cox did not want to drive the car. I think he was uneasy about driving on the right side of the road. Not your Daddy! He is a natural born driver and drove excellently, so he did all the driving during our time abroad. We toured through France and on the way saw the graves of the young boys who had been killed in the First World War. (Nearby was Rouen, where Daddy, Mammy, yourself and Francesca are on holiday at this very moment – 20$^{th}$ August 1984).

We continued our journey through France and by the time we got to Lyons, Daddy, Grandad and myself were so tired by the evening we decided to stay the night and went looking for an hotel. What a hope! Every place was full. Eventually we found an hotel which had just one bedroom vacant. I said:

"We must have two rooms. We have a 19-year old son."

The proprietor thought I was mad raising such an objection and then said that the room was a large one and he would put up a screen between the two beds. We were all so tired, we had to agree. I said to your Daddy

"You go up first," which he did. Eventually we went upstairs and as your Daddy did not speak to us we assumed he was asleep. I had just got into bed when I heard someone talking. I said to Grandad:

"Jack, we have a French man in this room. Get up and see where he is."

On investigation he found it was your Daddy talking in fluent French. We did not wake him.

On South again where we toured through beautiful country, we came within 23 miles of Monte Carlo. I said to your Grandad "Let's go there," but he would not, much to the disappointment of your Daddy and myself.

On to Spain – immediately we crossed the border I knew I was not going to like it. The smell from the sewage was awful. On again, and by the evening your Daddy was getting very tired and asked if we could stay at the next hotel we saw. I said "of course" and was I glad we did.

Spain does not have a warning of approaching night like we have, and when we got out of the car we discovered your Daddy had been driving along a road which was high and no protection at the side. We could quite easily have had an accident. The place was Arenys de Mar and it was a nice hotel, and it was quite comfortable.

After breakfast on the veranda we set off again, this time to Barcelona, a few miles further on. We stayed there and had some refreshment and I went to buy the *Woman* magazine and when I took it back to the car I could not find my spectacles. I only needed them for reading in those days. On telling your Grandad he said that we would go back to Arenys de Mar. I said it didn't matter as we could collect them on our return journey as I would not be reading very much. We were 23 miles from Sitges. He said "No" again and turned the car round. As soon as he turned the car I found my spectacles on the floor of the car and said it was all right now and we could go on to Sitges.

I remember now why my spectacles were on the floor. I was the navigator and was reading the map. We turned round again and a few miles further on we saw a beach and a lot of people sitting on it. I think your Daddy had had enough of driving and asked if we could stay there. It was Callela de la Costa and we booked into a very nice hotel and thought we would settle there for a few days. We stayed a week.

Your Daddy quickly undressed and got into his swimming trunks and lay on the beach. He lay face-down and like the fool that I am, I did not realise the sun was so hot and did not cover his back with a towel and consequently he got severe sunburn and was in pain for a week. He found consolation in swimming under water as I had bought a snorkel on the way down.

We thought we had been lucky being allocated front bedrooms looking onto the sea until we were awakened in the early hours of the morning by the sound of trains going to Barcelona.

We were the only British people in the hotel; the remainder were Germans. We must have been like the opera "Box and Cox" because being British we were up at an early hour of the morning when the Germans were coming back after being out all night, and as we were out during the day, the Germans were sleeping.

I did not like Callela de la Costa, nevertheless, I was surprised when Grandad Cox told us we would be moving on Monday to make our way home. I said this was nonsense as we had not to be in Calais until Saturday morning.

On the way a few miles further on we saw a sign pointing the way to Lloret de Mar and your Daddy had just turned the wheel to go there when once again Grandad Cox said "No."

I was very annoyed because all the arrangements had been left to me and thinking we were going to stay some time in Spain, much of the foreign currency was in Spanish money and I was left with a considerable amount of Spanish money which I now had no use for. One thing I was thankful for was that I had bought your Daddy a very expensive wrist watch (which he has to this day) as he celebrated his 20th birthday while we were away.

On again towards France, but before we crossed the border there was an expensive hotel and I said:

"We might as well lunch here and spend some of this Spanish money."

The meal was marvellous – steak and salad – and your Daddy had two helpings.

Then on to France where we had to exchange our Spanish money into Francs. I was FURIOUS when your Grandad went to the bank and I found out that in English currency we were given six shillings and eight pence in the pound. We lost a lot of money on this exchange and to make matters worse we had to wait two days in Calais before we could sail home. I can tell you, Dominic, your Grandad was not very popular with me at that time. However, as neither of us could be annoyed with each other for any length of time, all was soon forgiven, but not forgotten.

I am going to break off here because I want to tell you about the wonderful day I spent at your Nana's and Grandad's bungalow.

## 27TH AUGUST 1984

It is Bank Holiday Monday, 27th August 1984 and I want you to know about the wonderful day I had yesterday. We are approaching your 8th birthday on 5th October and my 86th on 7th October.

As you have a very good memory you will remember that I suffer from arthritis in both knees and cannot walk without aid. Your Nana and Grandad were wonderful to me. Your Mammy and Grandad came for me at a quarter to ten to take me to your Nanas, and your Daddy was there to greet me, having just got back from Church. I was welcomed with a cup of tea and a bacon 'butty'. It was lovely. I don't have a big appetite these days but on Sunday I excelled myself, eating three Yorkshire Puddings with lovely onion gravy and roast beef and baked potatoes, followed by raspberries and fresh cream and a waffle.

I had a beef sandwich at teatime and your Nana packed a huge sandwich for my lunch on Monday.

During talks with your Daddy I learned he had already told you about our trip to Spain and he has no doubt he told you other things I have written about, but never mind, you can read this to Francesca.

Before our holiday in Spain things took their normal course until 1956 when Grandfather Cox shocked me by asking:

"Would you mind if I went to Cyprus for a year?"

"Will you explain?" He said:

"Crown Agents are asking for ex-police sergeants and ex-army officers to act as warders in the Central Prison in Nicosia." I said:

"Is that what you want to do?" He said: "Yes". So I said:

"Go ahead and do it."

He did, and set off for Cyprus on 16th November. (I must explain that Grandad had once been Acting Sergeant temporarily but retired as a Police Constable). Your Great-Grandma Kilcullen took his departure with more sadness than I did. There was a great love between them and she kept saying:

"I wish I could see my 'son' just once more." I said:

"He has not gone for good. He will be home in November and then we will have a party."

Alas, it was not to be, for she died on 1st February 1957. Her birth date was 27th January 1875, but before she died she received a letter from Grandad Cox enclosing £4 to buy a bottle of whisky and saying how much he loved her, and said he loved her better than he did his own mother, as she had been kinder to him. I was so thankful she received this letter before she died.

Once again your Daddy proved his true worth. He sent a cable to his father and made all the arrangements for the funeral. Your Grandad wanted to come home but I said that he had to keep to his contract. I might have regretted this because he could have been killed. He was detailed to convey a prisoner, which necessitated going along Lederer Street (nick-named Murder Mile). The Governor sent for your Grandad and asked:

"Can you type, Cox?"

to which he replied:

"Yes Sir."

The Governor said he wanted some depositions typed and another man would have to take his place. That poor man was killed.

Grandad Cox served the full year in Cyprus and returned home in November 1957. Things soon became normal again.

Before he went to Cyprus he worked in the Records Offices, but there wasn't a vacancy when he came back, so he went to work for Colonel Ware who was Coroner for York. It was supposed to be part-time and the pay was low, so when he received a letter from the Civil Service asking if he would accept a vacant post, he was pleased to accept. For a while he worked in the library, handing out books, until he was transferred to the Royal Army Pay Corps Services. He enjoyed working there until he reached the age of 65 and then received a Retirement Pension; but I worked until I was 69. He did not like me working so long but I enjoyed my work and wanted to stay. Finally, he said:

"Enough is enough," and it was time I retired, which I did in January.

In October 1965 we moved from 57 Seventh Avenue to 24 Ashley Park Road, a bungalow which was quite small and totally inadequate. By this time of our living in the bungalow your Daddy met and fell in love with your beautiful Mammy. (I fell in love with her also and still love her to this very day). Your Daddy asked Grandad Bristow's permission to marry, which he gave on condition that they did not marry until your Mammy was 20 years of age. They became engaged to marry on her 18th birthday. We celebrated by drinking champagne at the bungalow, then went to the Fauconberg at Coxwold where we had a marvellous meal and your Great-Grandmother Carruthers was there. She was a wonderful lady and loved your Daddy from the first time of meeting him. This love was reciprocated because he loved her very much. Unfortunately and tragically Grandad Cox did not live to see your Mammy and Daddy married.

It was a very splendid wedding and your Nana and Grandad spared no expense for the reception – a sit-down meal, champagne, etc. The owner of the caterers who provided the food also acted as Master of Ceremonies, looking elegant in a red jacket. Incidentally, he was a friend of your Grandad and his name was Billy Duff. Prince Curtis, a wrestler from Honolulu came to York specially for the wedding and had to leave the reception early to catch an aeroplane for Singapore. I will not dwell on this subject, as your Mammy and Daddy can tell you about it.

Came the great day when you were born. What rejoicing! What a lovely party we had at your house following your Baptism. We all wanted to hold you, but I think Great-Grandma Carruthers won.

Later Francesca was born and again there was a party after her Baptism and rejoicing. Had your Mammy and Daddy asked me to choose names for you both I would have given you both the names with which you were christened. I have asked your Mammy and Daddy to give my Benemerenti Medal which I received from the Pope to Francesca.

When I was 16 years of age my beloved father gave me some advice which I have remembered all my life:

"Enjoy yourself but don't forget you are a lady".

To you, my beloved Dominic, I say:

"Enjoy yourself but don't forget you are a gentleman".

God Bless,

    Your loving Grandma,

        Elizabeth Margaret Cox

            (née Kilcullen) x

# THE WILLIAM EDWARD MEAKIN STORY

## BY

## WILLIAM MEAKIN

William Meakin aged 23

# INTRODUCTION

This amazing autobiography is written by a man who had only a basic education up to the age of fourteen years, but he was a very practical "hands-on" person as far as gardening and horses were concerned.

Bill's story tells the tale of how he grew up on his grandfather's farm in Liverpool up to the age of five, before returning to his ever-growing family in order to go to school. As a young man he helped his father in his smithy before becoming a farrier in the Army.

Written on scraps of paper, found after his death in 1985, Bill has recorded a variety of his life's experiences. In one line he modestly says that it was his job to see that all the horses which the Army took to the coronation of King George VI were in tip-top condition for the parade. Anyone who knows about horses will realise what an understatement of hard work and responsibility that was.

In 1921 Bill met and courted my mother's eldest sister, Rose Evelyn Pritchard who, according to my mother was "dance crazy" at that time. She was attracted to Bill because he was an excellent dancer as well as being a handsome soldier. They married in 1922 by special licence when he was on leave in York but, at the age of 18, Evie was considered by the Army to be far too young to accompany her husband when he had to return to his military duties abroad, so she continued working in the Cardboard Box Department at Rowntree's chocolate factory until permission was given for her to join him in India several years later.

There are brief references to Bill and Evie's children. My mother was of the opinion that they started their family in England with the birth of their son, Raymond, in 1930, but very little is written about their offspring. Raymond also went into the Army as a career soldier and reached the rank of Major. He survived both parents but died in 2007.

The ups and downs of Bill's life and achievements, although simply written, are well worth reading. He had a remarkable memory. He was a wonderful man, and I am grateful to him and my cousin Derek Meakin, (his only surviving son) for giving me the opportunity to share this story with a wider audience than just his close family.

# THE WILLIAM EDWARD MEAKIN STORY

by

## William Edward Meakin (1900-1985)

(Opened and concluded by his son Derek Meakin (1935 – )

*All of this story was found on hand-written pieces of paper amongst my Dad's effects, which was a very nice surprise.*

## PAGE 1

I was born at 99 Greenwich Road, Aintree, Liverpool, on 29th April 1900.

I did not know anything about the first three years of my life, being so young, but in later years I learnt a good bit about it from my mother.

We lived in a house on the corner of 3rd Avenue at the back and above a little shop which sold sweets, soft drinks, tobacco, matches, and bundles of chips for lighting fires. Early in 1903 we got a house in the avenues of Fazakerley, No. 19 Third Avenue. It was a lot nearer to where my Grandfather West lived with my Aunty Florence in Barlows Lane.

There was another sister born after we had moved house (Dorothy). So to make it easier for my mother, I was taken to my Grandad's little farm in Barlows Lane. His house was right at the bottom of the lane close to the railway goods-line, on a high embankment, and the lane went under the bridge, towards the racecourse. Well, I had two years there before I was called back home to start school when I was five years old.

## PAGE 2

During my stay with my Grandad and Aunty Flo, which I really enjoyed, I helped by feeding the chickens, ducks and geese, collecting eggs, and filling up the drinking fountains with fresh water. Grandad's dog, Bob, was my good friend. We went all over together.

Grandad had a yoke to carry a couple of big buckets of fresh water every other day from the next farm where the Barlow family lived in a big long thatched cottage. All the buildings were whitewashed. They had cows, horses, carts, ploughs, and more.

At the gate they had a load of quicklime, rough and green, which they put on the fields. This farm was half-way down the lane on the right. I used to help with the water, so Grandad made me a little yoke and two buckets, of which I was very proud. I didn't lose much water on the way back.

## PAGE 3

I used to sit on the plough on a cushion while Grandad ploughed the ground. When he had done enough he would couple the horse up to the harrow, the one with the spikes.

I learnt a lot of things about gardens, wild flowers, birds, and herbs. Grandad was a big believer in herbs. He had bunches of herbs hanging up in the house where the milk and water was kept. There were also some in the barn where there was hay, grain and potatoes, and a cart, a blue one. I also learnt about bees – the hard way. I got stung on the top of my head when I was watching Grandad change the combs for full ones. He fitted me out with some proper protection, so I was much safer after that.

## PAGE 4

Of course, that was a summer time job, but in the winter he had to feed them with thick sugary water. The honey was mainly apple blossom and clover, which tasted quite plain. After we had our tea and honey we had to chew a piece of tansy, which was a bitter taste, so it brought out the sweetness of our tea.

In the evenings before I went to bed my Aunty Flo would light the paraffin lamps. I used to think how cosy it was in the lamp light while

Grandad sat in his chair smoking his pipe in which he used to smoke a concoction of herbs that smelled really nice. After a while my Aunt would send me off to bed. I had to go to bed at 6.30 pm. I felt warm, snug and safe in that bed. The railway at the back of the house was about eighty yards away and, listening to the trains puffing up the slope, I soon fell fast asleep.

## PAGE 5

The next sound I would hear, was the cockerel – ours – then those on other farms. Then all the dogs would start the all-clear for the day.

With me getting a bit older, thoughts of school were beginning to creep in. When we had a lot of rain, the bottom of Barlows Lane by the railway bridge would be flooded and the geese and ducks used to spend nearly all day in the water. Even Bob, Grandad's dog, would wallow in it. There were plenty of wild birds to be seen all around the area, and I watched and learnt about them from my Grandad. As well as birds there were trees, flowers, grasses and animals. It was a lot to take in for a four-year old.

## PAGE 6

I have never forgotten what my Grandad taught me. The dog, Bob, went each morning for the daily paper. He would rush across the meadow in a straight line to the wall by the main road, then cross over to the shop, which was also the Post Office. Mr Richardson had the paper ready, and off Bob would go, over the road, over the four-foot wall in one bound, and back to the house in no time at all. He always got a little bit of fussing for being so obedient. I know he liked being fussed over. He never went into the house and was content just to lie on the step, just as if he was awaiting orders.

Well it was getting closer to Christmas 1904, and that meant me going back home, not an easy thing for me to do.

## PAGE 7

I came back home to the family, which was getting bigger every two years, and we all went to spend Christmas dinner with my other Grandad (Meakin). There were four of my uncles, two aunts, and Grandad, who was a wheelwright.

My uncles were called Roger, Joe, Henry and Sidney. My aunts were Sarah and Edie. I didn't see a lot of Aunt Edie. She went to live in London after she got married.

My father and Uncle Roger were blacksmiths. They owned a shop/smithy and were brought up there.

In my Uncle Roger's family there were fourteen children and two adults – sixteen – quite a crowd! In ours there were five at that time. It was an old house solidly built with Yorkshire stone flags on all the downstairs floors (scrubbed white). It was a roomy place and we had to use two rooms for all of us to sit down to dinner.

After dinner Uncle Henry took us all over the road to a little sweet shop and bought us all sweets (just the children). I think the lady in the shop had expected such a visit and had opened the shop specially.

## PAGE 8

There was a pub next to the shop and one next to Grandad's smithy. In years past they were stopping places for the stage coaches from Manchester, so the pubs were well patronised. They changed the teams of horses there.

In the smithy my Dad shoed most of the trotting horses that attended the trotting meeting at the bottom of Seeds Lane, where the trotting ground was. From there we would go to Barlows Lane, to my Mother's Father and Aunty Flo. She would have our Christmas tea ready. I think we were more relaxed there, and enjoyed it more.

When night time came, my family would all go home but leave me to stay at Grandad's. It was dark going home up the lane but Grandad West and the dog, Bob, would go with them to the main road, and they would be back in no time. By the time they had returned I would be fast asleep, snug in bed. Bob was never tied up at night. I liked that idea and so did he.

Boxing Day was no different to any other day. The cocks started it off. In 1904 there was plenty of snow about. I was glad Mum and Dad got home before it started.

## PAGE 9

In another week it would be 1905. I was learning a lot from Aunty Flo and Grandad, which had to come to its end. By the time of my 5$^{th}$ birthday in April I was back at home, No. 19 Third Avenue, ready to start school. I didn't know whether I would like it or not.

Anyway Mother took me to school, into the Infants, and after seeing the Headmistress left me to get on with it. It was very strange being in a classroom after the last two years in open places. Dinner time came and my older sister (Mabel) collected me at the door and we ran off home for our dinner, about a mile. Mother said:

"Well, Willie, how was school?"

"Not bad." I said "But I'm not going back."

After dinner I was soon bundled off back with my sister, like it or not. I found out I could not do as I liked. So I soon began to enjoy it.

## PAGE 10

The Infants' classes had little gardens in the playground area. They were all about six foot square and edged with bricks to keep them tidy. I liked doing the garden because of all that Grandad had shown me, so we kept ours nice and tidy.

I planted a young sycamore tree in the garden, and long after I had left school I went back to see it. It had certainly grown well. I suppose it would have been chopped down long ago! It would have been nice to know.

We had a lovely teacher (Miss Waite). I could do nothing wrong for her. I got on all right and was always in the fore with my drawing and painting; and I still keep it up to this day (1984).

Two years in the Infants seemed to fly, and we all looked forward to our summer holidays.

## PAGE 11

The weather was always nice and hot in those days and we all (the family) looked forward to our annual visit to the seaside at Ainsdale. That's where we spent our annual holiday for one glorious day of the year. We would all walk two miles from Fazakerley to Aintree station. It was the Cheshire lines railway. The baby (Charlie) was carried and the rest of us carried the food, drink in bottles, and the rest of the gear we needed.

The ride on the train was a treat in itself. The train went through the country to the sand hills by the shore, then along the coast to Southport. As soon as the train stopped at Ainsdale we all got off and admired the dark red painted engine before racing across the sand hills, which were about half a mile to the shore. At last sea, sand and lovely sunshine!

We all dashed about like mad on the beach and when everything was settled we got changed to go swimming – mainly splashing about in the waves. Later we would all get some food, then collect shells, pebbles and seaweed, ready for when we had to return home.

## PAGE 12

I am sure Mother and Father were enjoying it as much as us.

We would sit on the sand together for our lunch of sandwiches, cake and biscuits, and wash it all down with lemonade and ginger pop. Mother and Father drank tea. We would all play about, in and out of the sea, until it was time to make tracks for home,. Then all packed up, off we would go back to the station, but without the same dash as when we came.

We all trooped over the bridge to catch the train for Aintree. We soon collapsed into the seats once inside the carriage.

The evening was closing in by the time we arrived at Aintree station. The train driver waved to us all as we climbed the steps to the road. Another two miles and we would all be home again after a wonderful holiday.

# PAGE 13

We still had the rest of the school holidays to use up, especially with all that warm sun. It was a great time. We would talk about it for months, and then start looking forward to the following year.

By now I was eight years old and Father had got an allotment. A Mr Metcalfe had cows on the meadow and he moved them nearer to the station where he had a new shippen* built. The old homestead and outhouses were demolished. There was only a pond in the corner, with a group of trees around it left. Well into 1908 they started the allotments and my Father and I were the first to lift sods off the ground.

We had our work cut out skimming the sods off 88 square yards of meadow. It was all very good ground and every garden was taken over. The plots were all pegged out to keep the boundaries, which we marked with a wall of turfs all the way round.

We soon got it all turned over and started planting, seed and seedling potatoes, etc. The adults had formed a committee and members came round to see how everyone was getting on.

# PAGE 14

We had a good crop of everything and Mother saved a decent bit of money, not having to buy all the veg, and the family was still getting bigger.

I used to take papers around. I would start in the morning, at the station for 6.30 am, to collect the bundles of papers thrown off the guard's van. Myself and a couple of other lads, would carry them back to the shop – the Post Office part. The clerk would arrive about 7.55 am, but the rest of the shop had been open for hours, selling papers and cigarettes.

It did not take long for the lads to get off with their bags of papers. There were four lads, each with a different area to cover. So the job was done in plenty of time to get our breakfasts and on to school for 9 am.

---

\* A shippen (alternative spelling: shippon) is a dialect word for a cattle shed.

The boys were Sid Smith, Tommy Seymour, Walter Helsby, and myself. We would also wait for the 6 pm train for the Liverpool Echos and Expresses. We had our own rounds and customers waiting for their evening papers. Tommy had a long way to go – to Kirkby and Melling – so he went by bike. We all did very well for Christmas boxes from most of the customers.

Oh, by the way, the lady behind the Post Office grille was Miss Tindsley. It was now a lot closer to Christmas 1908 and New Year's Day, 1909.

## PAGE 15

There had been a lot of snow and ice which had lasted for weeks. Great big snowballs left on the pavement were too big to move any more.

There was a lot to be done on the allotment and it was a very cold job picking sprouts loaded down with snow and ice.

The winters were always very hard, but with luck it should be a lot better by Easter.

Everyone was pleased when Spring came along. My Dad said that all the gardeners were full of get-up-and-go, digging, planting, and generally tidying up. The warmer weather was magic.

I was now old enough to join the Scouts, which I did. I joined the 1st Liverpool. Their HQ was at or near Aintree station. It was a building that was used years ago for cock-fighting, a game that was stopped about 1850. All the spurs of these game cocks are in the Liverpool Museum.

The Emanuel Church was being built in Fazakerley and on completion they started a Scout Group. So I transferred to the 119th Liverpool Troop, after being two years with the 1st Liverpool Troop.

## PAGE 16

Our Scout uniform was very smart. We had fawn or navy-blue shirts, dark blue shorts, a red neckerchief around our necks, and a white lanyard with a whistle on it that went into our shorts pocket. We also had a waist belt and a knife on a belt swivel.

In 1910 the Scouts of Liverpool & District had a review parade in the fruit and veg. market (Casanue Street). We marched there and back in those days. The Patrol Leaders with their patrol flags, had lots of proficiency badges on their sleeves. The parade was for General Baden-Powell. He was the founder of the Boy Scouts. He had served in the Army in South Africa with the 5th Dragoon Guards. Also, every Sunday our troop held a Church Parade. Once a month a different troop was invited to come to the service and parade with us. Being a young troop we didn't have any bugles or drums.

Once a week Sid Smith and myself went to Church on Wednesdays to blow the bellows for the organist to do a little practising. For a couple of hours, we got sixpence each. It was good fun and two hours would fly past. We had choir practice on Tuesdays.

I was kept very busy each week, helping Dad on the allotment. Sometimes I would work on my own at the local chip shop, doing potatoes in a big drum that took the peel off. I did about a hundredweight every night.

# PAGE 17

I had to collect papers off the early trains and then deliver them before breakfast, and rush to school for 9 am.

Each dinner-time I would go to Mrs Jones' house to see if she wanted any messages done before I had my dinner. Then off to school at the gallop. I liked school fairly well, except for maths. I always got a bad report for maths.

At four o'clock I would be off again to the station for the evening papers to get them delivered. There was no rush then, but I did have to check to see if I was needed at the chip shop later.

While the evenings were long I spent a lot of time with Dad on the allotment. One day he said we could do with digging a well there. He marked it out and we started digging, putting the soil up one end of the garden out of the way. Then we came to lovely clean sand, which we kept in another pile. We got down quite deep, and my Dad was too big to get into the hole, so I took over. As I got much lower the water started to flow in and I had to roll my shorts up and take off my shoes and socks. It was quite cold at first but I soon got used to it. Every now and again Dad would lower a bucket to help remove most of the water. It was a long job, but worth the effort.

## PAGE 18

The next day the hole was nearly three-quarters full, so my Dad had found the right spot to dig. It took some time for him to empty the water out and put it on the garden, so I carried on and finished the job. To line the walls, we put holes in two barrels. I put stones at the bottom of the well and stood the first barrel on them. I packed it all round with sand to keep it straight and tight. Then Father pulled me out and we put the second barrel on top of it and packed that tight as well. When I'd finished, it was sticking up two feet above ground level so Dad made a square box with a lid on it, which could be locked up for when we weren't there, and he put that on top. We packed earth all round it until only about six inches of our well was showing above the ground. Thinking back on it, that must have been seventy years ago.

It was nearing Christmas again. It was much colder. We were all looking forward to what presents we may get for Christmas. A surprise for us all would be nice.

## PAGE 19

The present I got was a surprise to everyone. It was a ship's bugle! I woke everyone up at 4 am, standing on top of the landing, blowing my head off. I also think I woke most of the street. Later, we were all up, washed, dressed, and in our Sunday best. We always had our Christmas dinner at Grandad's where Aunty Sarah had everything set up. It was amazing to see how the family all got into the house – aunts, uncles, and cousins galore.

We were not allowed to go outside snowballing, because we all had our best clothes on. After a good day at Grandad's we would set off to visit my Mother's family in Barlows Lane, where Aunty Flo and Grandpa greeted us as though they had not seen us for years.

## PAGE 20

We all sat round in the lamp light, which had been lit early because of the short days. It seemed cosier to me because of the snow. Outside everything was covered with frost and snow, which sparkled in the light from the house.

It was a Saturday night, and a Christmas holiday, so instead of me going back home with the others when the time came for them to go, I was allowed to stay for a couple of days extra. I was soon snug and warm in my favourite bed, with all the noises of the farms in my ears.

Next morning the snow was quite thick and deep about the farm, and all the jobs still had to be done. So all the hens, ducks and geese that had survived the Christmas table had to be fed and watered, and all their water fountains had to be thawed out first, before being re-filled. Bob, Grandad's dog, was well looked after with lots of soft hay to keep him warm in his kennel. In another week it would be New Year 1911, so I would have to go home and prepare for school.

## PAGE 21

I made lots of pals with the lads in our class. Our teacher, Mr Steeper, was very strict, but a jolly good all-round teacher. There were about forty-eight boys in the class, but I can only remember forty-two of them. I have written their names down. I don't think many people could do that seventy-three years later.

We were always together through the years, class to class. But in 1911 I went into the Seniors, so we still all had a long way to go.

Every Wednesday we attended the school swimming baths, which was very exciting. We all marched to the baths. It belonged to the school, and the gym was built above it, so we didn't have far to get there. The teacher, each week, would say "Here's a shilling for the first one to swim a length of the baths."

I was determined to win that shilling, so I used to walk, every Saturday, four miles to Walton Church baths to train. It cost a penny to get in, and I stayed for about three hours. Anyway, the training paid off and I got my shilling. The following week about four more of the lads did it.

## PAGE 22

Later we all had to go in for our swimming certificates. They had us all keeping fit, doing lots of sports – some days swimming, other days athletics. Another day after dinner we would go over to Hartley's (Jam Factory) sports fields, to play football in the Winter and cricket in the Summer. We could rely on better summers those days. One of the lads would take the ball home until the next morning, then hand it back to the teacher.

When Easter came round we had a short holiday, and the weather was always bright, sunny and warm. Everyone was turned out in new clothes. The children all played games like whip-and-top, marbles and kites (home-made). I had an iron hoop that Father made at work, with a couple of steerers with it. We ran for miles in relays in teams of three. We would run two miles away and two miles back, then another mate would take over. We all enjoyed doing it and timed ourselves by the Post Office clock. We all slept well those days!

## PAGE 23

Also, my sisters would be out playing in their sunshine frocks. They had wooden hoops and sticks, not iron like us boys. They also had dolls and dolls' houses with furniture in, that Father had made for them.

Every Sunday night during the Winter, Mother would read to us, sitting round a big fire all nice and cosy. She would read from a paper called 'The Marvel' – serial tales about a fat boy called Billy Bunter. He had mates called Tom Cherry, a Chinese boy Wun Lung, and another lad whose father was in the diamond business in South Africa. These boys got up to lots of mischief. They were all good stories and Mother made them very interesting.

While Mother was reading, Father was smoking his Church Warden pipe – a clay pipe – about eighteen inches long. Us kids would take turns in lighting it because it seemed such a long way off from Dad.

## PAGE 24

By this time our family had grown. There was Jim, Mabel, myself, Charlie, Muriel and Mum and Dad. Oh, I remember another story Mother told us – called 'Wooley of the Wilds' – a Canadian tale of snowy wastes, wolves, snow shoes, sledges – and tales of all sorts of animals surviving the winters.

We were never tired of listening when Mother was reading. Oh, I forgot to say that while Mum was reading, the oven had been loaded up with scrubbed clean potatoes for our suppers. That always put a nice finish to the evening. Even the baby slept through it all.

The weather was getting a lot colder, so we were all quite satisfied to stay indoors and keep warm. Christmas was getting near again – and the snow! We all loved playing out in the snow, that was until we were all soaked and frozen, then it was a dash into the house to thaw out. But Mother always kept us in. She said "You've had enough for today." So that was that!

## PAGE 25

When the Winter arrived in earnest, it was a really hard job to get up early in the morning to get the papers from the train. I think we were all glad when the Christmas holidays came again because there were lots of other things to do.

We had lots of carol-singing nearly every night before Christmas Day. We used to sing about six carols before we dare knock on any door. We always got something. Some people would ask us inside to sing, especially if there was an elderly couple inside. Even going round with the papers, there were very few people that did not give us a Christmas box.

Christmas Eve arrived. That was the highlight for us. Reveille was at 4 am because I had the bugle under my pillow. I've had a good laugh about it ever since. I'm sure my Mother and Father even expected it, that early morning bugle call, only one day a year.

## PAGE 26

We always had a nice New Year. In 1912 we had a party for family and friends. We played all kinds of games and Mother made the supper of potato cakes, oat cakes, mince pies, and lots more nice food as well.

We all sang the New Year in and listened to the Church bells, train whistles, ships' hooters and sirens, which kept up for some time into the New Year. It was the longest party we ever had. I think everyone was the same. The next day was cold but bright, so we just carried on with our normal things that we had to do.

Back at school we had to settle down to our work and looked forward to Easter, and warmer weather.

The snow had all gone and things brightened up. There was plenty of work to do on the allotment so I helped Father as much as I could. We got on very well together.

Everyone admired the garden, for it was always neat and tidy. The paths were straight and all the rows of vegetables had been laid out with the aid of a line, all straight as a die.

## PAGE 27

I was always enthusiastic about my Scout meetings. I think that my Scout training has held me in good stead all these years. I used to organise all kinds of things for the troop. I passed my $1^{st}$, $2^{nd}$ and $3^{rd}$ class badges, and cycling, gardening, swimming, First Aid, signalling and cooking. I had quite an armful.

The choir took up part of the weekly activities, and Sunday Church Parade with the troop. Also my morning and evening paper rounds kept me very busy.

As the Summer was nearing, we were all looking forward to the flower and vegetable show at the allotments, when we would pick out the best of the veges and flowers. My Father always got a couple of prizes, at least for his favourite potatoes.

There were also all kinds of sports at the show which was held at the trotting ground at Aintree, at the corner of Seeds Lane and Melling

Road. They had contests for bunches of wild flowers; drawings and paintings; bread making; jam making, etc. Everyone enjoyed it.

The other nice thing we looked forward to was our annual holiday trip to Ainsdale, for the sea and sand. That was our highlight of the year.

## PAGE 28

The cricket season was about over, so I was back to football at school amongst all the lads. I was very keen on football and on some Saturdays I forgot to go home.

One day Mother told me to go for a loaf of bread. It was a Saturday and I met some of the lads with a ball. They asked: "Are you coming for a game, Bill?"

I soon ended up on the pitch and played football all day. Some of the lads went home for their dinners and came back again but I stayed on until about 6 pm. When I arrived home Mother, looking mad, said: "Where's the bread?"

I put my hands in my pockets and brought out the money. I said that I was only playing football. Of course, I got a good belting for it, and that was that.

As the weather was getting cooler and the days shorter, we did more running games, mainly to keep warm. With the days being shorter, we spent more time indoors. At one time I was helping Jim, my eldest brother, to construct parts for a wireless. He was four years older than me. I looked up to him, for he had a good mechanical mind. I learnt a lot from him. He had quite a lot of spare parts, and we enjoyed fiddling with them all.

## PAGE 29

The allotment looked a bit bare since most of the vegetables and flowers had finished, except for the hardy Chrysanths; they were always at their best late in the year. There was plenty of tidying up to do. When it came, the frost would do the sprouts and celery some good, parsnips as well. The rhubarb would be dug up, to winter out of the ground.

The family did well out of the garden and there were plenty of potatoes and cabbages, etc. Every Sunday for tea, during the Winter, we had a great big piled up plate of potato cakes, well-buttered. They were great. I still have them now, I just can't get out of the habit. Some habits are hard to break.

Well, it was getting near Christmas again. Everyone was looking forward to it with great anticipation especially us kids. By now there were eight children in the family. Enid and Fred (twins) were born on 3rd August 1912, so the family was getting bigger.

## PAGE 30

Halfway through the month, and the snow had arrived. It was cold. Lots of people grumbled about it, but us children all enjoyed it. We stayed out late carol singing, wet and snow-covered, but we still got invited into houses to sing. After we had made some money we packed up for the night. The money we made all went to buy presents for the family. They were only small presents, but given with good heart.

The usual things happened at Christmas. Stockings hanging at the bottom of the bed – all of us waiting to see Father Christmas with one eye open – but it didn't work. As normal, I would wake everyone up at 4 am with my bugle call. We all opened our stockings and messed about a bit, then by 5 am we were all fast asleep again.

After breakfast we would get ready to visit our two Grandparents and families. Uncle Henry, as always, took the kids for sweets, and by now there were plenty of us. When our dinners had settled we would get packed up and walk the two miles, whatever the weather, to Grandad West's house in Barlows Lane.

## PAGE 31

First of all we said "Happy Christmas" to Grandad and Aunt Florrie then we all huddled around the big fire that was roaring away in the sitting room. More presents were passed around with great excitement, then when we had calmed down we would have our tea. Aunty Flo was a very good cook and she had made a lot of everything we liked to eat.

Grandpa sat in his chair smoking his pipe of herbal tobacco, which smelled really nice. Then later we would sing carols and songs. Grandad's home-made wine was drunk. That was made from different herbs, flowers and berries.

Soon it was time to go home. It went over very quickly. I asked if I could stay for a few days and was told "Yes." All the kids went outside to see Bob before they went home.

## PAGE 32

After a week's stay I had to go back home. Mother was always glad to have me back with the family, where we were all very close, and I enjoyed it.

We had celebrated the New Year at Grandpa's. Now it was 1913. Everything was back to normal. School started. Trains were running. The trams had it rather bad with the snow, and the salt car had not made too much impression on the roads – only in the centre of the roads where the tram-lines were.

The horses and carts which were coming in from the country with potatoes and vegetables had a heavy time along the slippery snowy roads. Those days the weather always changed for the good, and most things would soon be back to normal.

Once I started school I really enjoyed it, which got me thinking about all the school friends I had known over the years. So I shall write some names down:

*INFANTS 1905 – 1907*
*Miss Waite and Miss Gwyn*

*JUNIOR MIXED 1907 – 1910*
*Miss Grease, Miss Keats,*
*Phoebe Beverage, Lewis Orme, Minnie Currie, Amy Williams,*
*Margaret Williams*

### SENIORS – 1910 – 1914

*Mr Steeper's class, Longmoor Lane School*

| | | |
|---|---|---|
| John Beasley | Eric Linsley | Henry Caldwell |
| James Arrowsmith | Douglas Gorton | James Scott |
| Joseph Critchley | Henry Jagues | Samuel Davis |
| Stanley Holden | Norman Price | Frank Maudsley |
| Frank Ross | Phillip Crane | Cecil Pinfold |
| Bill Fowler | Norman Pearson | Harold Letchford |
| Lennon Fowler | Lesley Crone | Fred Bowman |
| Peter Brown | Tim Waring | Tommy Seymour |
| Walter Brown | Derwent Sharp | Hector McDonald |
| John England | Albert Kidson | Bill Meakin |
| Hartley Rushton | George Sanderson | Harold Hilton |
| Frank Capstick | Joseph Stow | Norman Leitch |
| Hector Stevenson | George Disley | Reg Watling |
| | | George Downing |

Not a bad memory, after SEVENTY years.

## PAGE 33

It was now 1914, a bad year for me because my school days had come to an end. It was also an exciting year because I had to start looking for a job. I started work in May in the foundry at Chatburns. Not good for a young lad, but a job with pay, so I bought myself a bike for three shillings and sixpence.

The First World War broke out in August, so the foundry was busy. Those who worked there were collected in a big van. The apprentices got their week's pay. All the men received double pay, My wage was four shillings and sixpence, with sixpence for hospital. So I had a gold half sovereign* the first and last I ever earned.

---

\* A sovereign was a former British gold coin worth £1. A half sovereign was worth ten shillings (50p in today's currency).

The next week a policeman and two Navy men called at our house. They said they wanted the wireless receiving set which my brother Jim and I had made. They even enquired around, to find out if we were Germans. We could not imagine such an idea! Anyway, we got a receipt for it and they said we could have it back after the war was over. Mum and Dad thought it was quite funny.

## PAGE 34

During the very early days of the war I spent all my extra time at Walton Town Hall which was the local recruiting office. After work I would get washed, put on my Scout uniform, and go to help out as best I could. It was a very busy place and I would be there until about eleven o'clock, then bike home.

Other Scouts went to help at the hospitals and there was a good number of them. There were tea wagons for the men who had signed on. They could get tea and food before they went off, so there was plenty of washing up to be done.

Everyone not in the Forces was working on munitions or some kind of work that would help the war effort. All the factories had changed over to war work. No-one was idle at all.

We lived well on the outskirts of Liverpool, at Fazakerley, and with a couple of miles to work and back, then on to the Town Hall to help out, and back home again, really kept me busy.

## PAGE 35

As the war progressed, things appeared to be running smoothly. That was just my impression! What did I know?

Ration books came out and everybody, it seemed to me, had to queue up for anything they wanted. There were queues everywhere. At weekends my brothers and sisters had to stand in line early in the morning to reserve a place for our Mother to buy her rations. These were not very much at the grocers or butchers, especially at the butchers.

Because we had the allotment it really helped out with veges and potatoes. Mother made sure some of the less fortunate people were helped out.

After a year working at Chatburns I left and went to the Signal Works as a fitter apprentice. The factory was closer to home. It only took me fifteen minutes to get there. I hadn't been there long when John Griffiths who was doing my cousin's work as my Father's mate at the smithy whilst he was serving in the war, took a job with a coal merchant. He enjoyed it so he stayed, and I got the job at the smithy.

## PAGE 36

I was now sixteen and very pleased to be working for my Father, for he had all the experience to help me, which made the job all the more interesting. I worked very hard, and my Father was very strict. I learnt all about horses, shoeing, harnesses, carts, wagons, and which tools to use. I also learnt to make tools for special jobs. Oh, I also had to learn about mending coal wagons that brought coal from the colliery.

It was not all fun, or easy, for I had a cart-horse, Clydesdale, stand on my big toe about five times in succession. My toe was like a squashed tomato. Another time I was working the fire and I had not cooled out the handling end of a bar of iron which Dad had turned round. I gripped it with both hands, and it stuck to me. I had no skin on my hands for a good while after. But it certainly taught me a lesson.

The day the war was over, everyone expected it at eleven o'clock. All the carts and horses were in the yard by eleven. Then hundreds of ships' hooters, horns, and train whistles set off blowing, and blew for what seemed the rest of the day. Everybody went mad, and all the trains and trams were full of what seemed to me, crazy people all having a FREE RIDE.

## PAGE 37

There were jubilations all through the night, and it was a treat to have the blackout finished after so long. When the street lights came on they shone bright and clear. It was all so hard to believe it was all over.

Towards the end of 1918-1919, all the soldiers returning from the war were demobbed back into Civvy Street. Those that had to leave or give up their jobs to serve in the war, were ready to get their jobs back. Well my Father said to me "I'm sorry, son, to lose you, but you'll have to let your cousin take his job back." So that was that, and I really liked working with Father in the smithy. By the end of August 1919, I was out of work.

On the first day of September I went off looking for blacksmith's jobs that were advertised in the local paper, The Liverpool Echo. I went for two interviews. At the first place the boss looked at me and said "Well, what can you do?" I told him "shoeing heavy horses, ironwork for carts and wagons, and hooping wheels." So he said "Well, that's good, I'll let you know later on. Leave me your address." So I did. I thanked him, then went off looking for the next job which was over the River Mersey at Birkenhead.

## PAGE 38

After a little hunt around I found the place, also the boss, and he asked me all the same questions as the previous employer did. And I got the same answer from him! After leaving my address, etc., I walked back to the ferry boat and crossed the river back to Liverpool. I wandered around town for a while until I came upon a recruiting office for the Army at the corner of Hay Market. So putting my best foot forward, I went in. I found a couple to Sergeants of two different regiments there, both looking very smart, but staring at me. One was infantry, the other cavalry. The first one said "Well, son, you're just the sort of fellow I want in my regiment." He said it was the Lancashire Fusiliers.

I looked at him and said: "I've come to join a horse regiment." So the other Sergeant said "Come over here, son. You want my regiment, it's the $5^{th}$ Royal Irish Lancers." I was thunderstruck! I said "Well, you can put me down for them, as long as there are horses."

## PAGE 39

What happened next was quite amazing to me. I was sworn in and enrolled there and then. Papers were made out, warrants, and ration tickets for my departure to Canterbury Cavalry Barracks the next day were issued. I was highly delighted and could not get home quick enough to let my Mother know.

My Father had not left work at that time. When he did come in, I told him, not sure what he would say. He said "Well, how did you get on, Will?" I said I got a job and started the next morning. "What is it?" he asked. "I've joined the Army." It took him by surprise. Then he said "Well, son, you've made your bed, you will have to lie in it." Mother was a little upset, but the pair of them saw my point with the work situation.

Next day I said goodbye to all the family. I got the tram from Fazakerley to Lime Street Station and caught the 10 am train down to Canterbury.

## PAGE 40

This was the BEGINNING of a FRESH LIFE. I found a companion on the train. We were both joining up and going to the Barracks at Canterbury, so we both had company on the journey. His name was Walter Chritchley, from Aughton near Ormskirk. That's not too far from Liverpool. The two of us walked into the guards-room at about 5.30 pm.

It was quite a shock to the system, all the different kinds of training we all had to do, but first we had to get fit. I already thought I was, but got proved differently much to my amazement. When fit we started to learn about the horses, which was a very good subject for me. I had no problems with them, but a lot of the recruits did. We got sorted into troops and were billeted above the stable blocks. In those days that was our central heating system.

Things were settling down and we started doing sword drills and lance drills, and this was before any of us had sat on a horse. All the thrills and spills came later when we entered the riding school. The effect was plain to see. Thinking back, it was a great laugh for some of us.

After the initial training we were put into our trades, of which mine was blacksmithing. I settled into it eagerly. The Farrier Sergeant was well satisfied with my work; so was I. Of course, looking after the horses was the main priority and kept us extremely busy.

We also had to fit in education classes, and all the drills. When we'd finished for the day we spent most of our time cleaning our kit and ourselves.

# PAGE 41

The Regiment left Canterbury for India at the end of 1919. We boarded the ship *Manitou*. It had been taken off the Germans at the end of the war. It was quite a voyage. I can remember the great time we had when we crossed the Equator. It wasn't a very big pool on board, especially for all the troops on the ship, but we had a Father Neptune event, and quite a lot of people got very wet.

When we arrived at Bombay we were marched to the railway station then put on a train. We didn't find out where we were going until our journey had got going. The word went round, it was to Risalpur, a really long train journey.

Conditions were now very different for us all. The older soldiers helped us young ones to cope with the heat and dust and people. We took over from the 11th Hussars, and their horses were in tip-top condition, which made our life a little easier. By now I was in the 1st Troop A Squadron, 5th Royal Irish Lancers, at Risalpur, North West Frontier Post, India.

# PAGE 42

It was very hot and dusty at the North West frontier We had to do patrols up to the Khyber Pass, watching for renegade tribesmen. I always got the feeling that they were watching us! The patrols took a lot more out of the horses than us troops.

In the barracks I was getting on very well with the older soldiers, most of whom were Irish men, as it was a well-known Irish Regiment. They would ask me to read their letters to them and in some cases, to write letters for them. So in helping out like this, I got on very well with them all, to the point where they trusted me to look after their money, because they didn't want to spend it all on drink, gambling and women. So I held all their money in the chest at the end of my bed. It was not locked, for I knew no-one would touch it, as everyone's money was in it. And it was very successful.

In 1921 I had become a good soldier and farrier. I really enjoyed my life in India very much.

Then we were told bad news – that we had to return to the UK because Regiments, as we knew them, were to be amalgamated. It was a very sad time for us all. We came home not knowing what the future had in store.

I then got my chance to return to Liverpool on leave, which was marvellous. I had a new brother when I got home. Alan was born on 6$^{th}$ March 1921. That brought the family up to ten children.

## PAGE 43

I was very disappointed because I had to leave my Regiment. I was transferred into the Inniskilling Dragoon Guards, and posted to York. My new Regiment had also been amalgamated with the 5$^{th}$ Dragoon Guards but they did blend into one Regiment for a very long time.

York turned out to be special for me because I started courting Rose Evelyn Pritchard. We were married on 22$^{nd}$ September 1922 at St. Cuthbert's Church, Peaseholme Green, York. The Church was almost opposite to my new wife's father's pub, namely The Leeds Arms. It was next door to the Black Swan, which was well-known for two bits of history. Number one: General Wolfe lived there before his battles in Canada. Number two: After the house became an Inn, Dick Turpin had stayed there. He was caught fleeing over the rooftops, then was imprisoned at York, before being hanged on the gallows at the Knavesmire.

Rose and I had our honeymoon at Scarborough, for a week. Then it was back to York Cavalry Barracks to catch up with my mates and my horses. But before long I was on my travels again with the Regiment. It was going to be very hard this time, because Rose would not be able to come with me right away.

## PAGE 44

The 5th Inniskilling Dragoons arrived in Gibraltar and took over from the Staffordshire Regiment, which had to go to Iraq. There was trouble there. We took over Beauna Vista Barracks, overlooking the bay and entrance to the Mediterranean Sea. It was a spectacular place and the climate was lovely and warm.

We did not have any parades, except for gym. It was optional how we did gym, so our squadron went swimming. It wasn't really a pool, but a circular inlet in the rocks. It was quite deep, and there was a springboard. Everyone enjoyed it and took plenty of snaps with their cameras.

The Barrack rooms were rotten with bugs. We all put our iron beds outside and set them on fire to kill the bugs in the tubing, and we laid the blankets out in the sun, so it reduced the bugs a lot.

We toured the rocks and caves all over Gib. Lots of the caves were full of food. Others were full of ammunition of every calibre, even for the big guns on the Rock.

## PAGE 45

On the South side of The Rock, there was a water shed which caught all the water for supplies to the town, and the different Barracks of which there were three, ours, Casmate, and the Central Barracks in the town.

The troops in the Town Barracks had to look after all the apes on The Rock and feed them. The apes used to sit on each side of the gateway to the town, just like sentries, waiting for people to give them food. It is the only place in Europe where there are apes. It was said that if the apes left The Rock, Britain would lose it.

There was only one level place there, and that was the parade ground. It was also the football and hockey pitch used by the Army, Navy, Air Force, and all the people in the town. All the things in the shops were tax-free, including beer and spirits. Quite a lot of the lads took full benefit of that, which led to them having thick heads the next day. Me? Well, I was teetotal!

Sunday was Church Parade. There were not many exceptions. The Army and Air Force were on it, and whatever ships' crews that happened to be docked. It was always a great sight and, to me, a thrill to be on it.

## PAGE 46

We took over the little forge (smithy), from a couple of Garrison Artillery chaps. Neither of them had any idea about shoeing, so they bowed out gracefully.

All they had been doing was that one of them would go to the sea-wall to fish in the sea, then take his catch back and put it in the trough by the fire. The other chap would peel the spuds and make chips. Then the fish was killed, and it was fish and chips all round. That was the reason for all the spud peelings in one corner, and all the bits of fish and bones in another place. What a smell! Well, we soon put paid to that, and had the place ship-shape and sparkling.

The Governor had two ponies in his stable, so I sent one of my lads to bring one over to the smithy. I must say I was shocked by the state of its feet – down at heel and up at the toes.

The poor thing looked as if it was on rockers. I set to work and trimmed its feet up, and got them back to their natural state and shape; then I made it a nice new set of well-fitting shoes. I think even the pony knew the difference.

## PAGE 47

I treated two more ponies in the same manner, so they all looked a hundred per cent better. The Governor was highly delighted and thanked us all for our kind efforts. He spoke to our CO about it. The Governor hardly used the ponies, so during the rest of our stay on The Rock I didn't have to shoe them again before we left for Egypt.

In the meantime, we all enjoyed ourselves in the town or on the shore, but mostly in the water. On the flats, as it was called, there was a tree with one half lemons and the other half oranges, something I have never seen before or since. There was also a big floral clock which struck the hour, and bells rang after each hour. It sounded good. At the edge of the flats was the harbour. It was amazing how close it was. There were a few trees near the gateway to the town. I think the apes enjoyed their shade, for most of them congregated there. It was a regular apes' meeting place.

## PAGE 48

The houses and shops in Gibraltar were all trim and clean, but there were plenty of young donkeys galloping about in the town, sort of playing.

It looked like some town in Algeria or Morocco. There were coloured awnings over the shop fronts, and even tables and chairs on the pavements, with sunshades over them. I think there were more tables outside, than in.

The pathway over to the Spanish mainland was closed to people without a permit. We hoped we might get a chance to visit, because we all wanted to visit a bullfight, but to our disappointment, we could not get any passes fixed up.

We enjoyed our stay on The Rock, especially the swimming. I suppose they were just getting us acclimatised, for we knew we were not staying, but would soon be on board a ship again, bound for Egypt.

## PAGE 49

Yes, our destination was Egypt. Helmieh Camp, about three miles from Cairo. It was August 1922, and very hot. We were really sorry to have left Gibraltar, but not its bugs!

We only had one Squadron, so the 'Skinns' were all kept together. We all soon mixed and got friendly, even though our cap badges were not the same. I have a photograph of one of the Regiment working near the bungalow, making one crest from the two separate Regimental badges.

It was getting closer to Christmas 1922, and we all got organised. Our forge staff was a lot bigger than expected, but we managed. There were about thirty mules in the lines to be allotted out. It was a big transport section.

The stables were very primitive, as were the bungalows, which reminded me of the cowboy films; no windows, just wooden shutters. They hardly had any rain out there, so with the climate being so warm, the roofs had feet on them, so as to leave a gap for any breeze to blow through. But it didn't help when the sand blew in.

## PAGE 50

The smithy was just the same, a long shed, with a line of uprights down the middle to hold the roof up. Fixed near the floor there were three separate strands of thick wire for tying the horses and mules. There was a fire and an anvil in each quarter, and a small section for the Farrier Major – and sand everywhere!

Out at the back, the sand-dunes stretched for miles. It was part of the desert that once was a forest. I think it was an area mentioned in the Bible. After the rains and floods, all the forest was petrified. There were still pieces of branches to be found. In the camp there were a few large pieces of fossilised tree trunks which rang like a bell when struck with a metal object, and the design of the bark on the trees was still to be seen.

Christmas time was getting very near. All the lads were quite excited about what it would be like to have Christmas out there in those very hot conditions. They hoped the sand would not blow up.

## PAGE 51

EGYPT HELMIEH CHRISTMAS 1922. The Regiment gave us all a lovely Christmas dinner. Most of the lads were rather wobbly afterwards, so they went to sleep it off. Those that could make it, returned in time to get some tea dished up to them.

Once a week some band members came onto the square to play to those who wanted to listen, but for Christmas, all the band turned out. They even brought their own seats to sit on. They also brought instruments, music sheets, and most of them had a dog, which usually sat under their seats while they played. Lots of the lads sat around enjoying the band's efforts, and some of them also had a dog.

The band played a couple of tunes. The next one was 'A whistler and his dog.' All was well until the end, when all the band pretended to bark. That's when all the dogs from the band and spectators started barking and fighting. Nobody could separate them. With sand and dust flying about it was a super performance, but shorter than expected. It still makes me laugh when I think about it.

# PAGE 52

It was another year on now, and we had quite a variety of parades and exercises to do.

At the other Barracks at Heliopalis, there were the 9th Lancers, and also the 8th Royal Irish Hussars. We had a combined exercise, further out into the desert. Our Regiment was to be against the 9th Lancers.

The General, as normal, was giving the exercise orders, and we, the Inniskilling Dragoons were facing a line of Lancers. Both Regiments were in open order. The trumpeter sounded the charge, expecting soon after, to sound the right-wheel. The General who was fully taken up with the spectacle, seeing the swords drawn at the engage, forgot to inform the trumpeter, so instead of turning right we all clashed.

Talk about Balaclava! There were horses and men all over the desert. Two horses died in a head-on clash. Two had broken legs, and lots of men were in a bad state. Sergeant Major Trimble helped to save one chap's life by sucking a blood clot from his throat. The General said: "It was the finest charge I have ever seen in my life." Well, it was all right for him, he was well clear.

## PAGE 53

After all the dust had died down and the injured were taken to hospital, our poor horses had to be sorted out. They had to be taken back to their stables. All injured horses went straight to the veterinary lines. Being the farrier, I had to shoot two horses, making four dead in total. They all had to be accounted for, that was the Army way. And it was my job to skin them, three of ours and one of the 9th Lancers.

I posted one man to stay with them, for fear of vultures. I later returned with my skinning knives and transport wagon to collect the skins and saddlery. It did not take too long. As I was finishing I noticed lots of vultures in a big circle, just waiting for us to move away before attacking the four carcases. Loaded up, we pushed off back to camp, and we almost missed our tea.

Some of the injured men were in hospital at Cairo for a short while, but at least they were not as badly off as those four horses.

## PAGE 54

Later in the year, as it got warmer, we had trips down the Nile to the first barrage. It's like a big dam, built to hold back the waters, so that the Egyptians could irrigate the country on both sides of the river. The country around the barrage had lovely gardens, full of palm trees, tropical plants, ferns and shrubs. They also grew my Grandad's favourites – spuds, carrots, sweet-corn, even wheat and cotton. We took with us plenty of food, fruit and drink (water).

I took my camera along with me and took plenty of snaps of the lads enjoying themselves. There were quite a number of dhows on the river. They looked very strange to us, with their large three-cornered sail, long mast, and diagonal style, which has been used for a long time – thousands of years, in fact.

Still with trips in mind, we all enjoyed visiting whatever we could. The pyramids and sphinx were great. We managed to climb one of the pyramids, which was quite amazing. Later we had our first ride on a camel. It was not as easy as riding a horse, but a good experience for us all. Cairo was also on the list to visit. I think my look around the Cairo museum was the most interesting place for me. I was in there for hours. Most of the lads had drink and other things on their minds.

## PAGE 55

In 1924 the Regiment left Egypt, but not through Port Said. We went by train to Port Tewfik, past the Bitter Lakes, to the South end of the Suez Canal. That was something everyone wanted to do. It was some trip across the Indian Ocean, but a nice time to relax, as there were no horses to bother about for a while.

It was now November and we all landed at Bombay, a very busy place with big white buildings and golden domes. But for us, there was no chance to look around. They soon had us all on the train to Bangalore in the Mysore Province. Bangalore was a really good Station (Barracks), well laid out, plenty of room for men and horses. As usual they gave us plenty to do: drills, courses, and patrols. The Mysore Province had wonderful countryside, very different from Egypt. Our smithy was always busy. We even had to try and teach the young subalterns to shoe horses.

At one stage the Regiment was sent to Madras where there had been some local trouble. It was about four hundred miles away, so we travelled about twenty miles a day. Eventually we marched into Madras or, in our case, rode in covered in dust, with flags flying and the mounted band playing. We stayed long enough to make sure things had cooled down. The British Navy also turned up in port, which brought on plenty of competition.

## PAGE 56

The Regiment returned to Bangalore by train, which was a good thing for us and the horses.

Later in 1924 we all moved, horses as well, to Risalpur, and we took over from the 1st King's Dragoon Guards. I was quite happy with the move as I had been at 'Rissy' before with the 5th Lancers. 'Rissy' (as we all called the place) was near Peshawar. Our train journey took about a week.

We spent four years at Risalpur. It was a good camp, and we improved it as time went on. Life was a lot easier in India, because we all had natives doing all our chores, from keeping us cool (punka wallah), cooking (bobbogy), cleaning our shoes (bearer), doing our laundry (dhobi wallah) and gardening (marlih wallah). In the smithy the native helpers also had names such as (narlebund wallah) for the shoeing smith, (syce) a groom; (moochi) a shoe-maker, but not the same shoes as I made for the horses. My job as a farrier kept me very busy, mainly because horses' shoes did not last long in the conditions of the local countryside.

## PAGE 57

After five years apart in 1927 my wife Rose, who preferred to be called Evie, arrived in India. We went up to 'Rissy'. It was a magical feeling for us both. We were allocated a married family's bungalow which was very plain but to us it was our very first home. Evie settled in very well. She took to Army life better than a lot of the troopers.

At last we started to enjoy our married life together. We soon had her riding the horses. We had plenty of good days out riding in the hills around Kantspur. We even hired some local Jat* horses. They were safer to use in that terrain.

Evie had certain scary moments in the bungalow, such as "big rats like small dogs", she said. We had to keep our food high up to keep the rats away because they would dip their tails into bottles and jugs. Not nice! Also there was the occasional snake to brush out; but none of it put her off enjoying India.

## PAGE 58

At the beginning of 1928 Evie found out she was pregnant, which was wonderful news, but not easy for her because of the heat conditions.

---

\* Jat = A member of an Indo-Aryan people of the Punjab and Uttar Pradesh

Also, I was not there all the time, but the other married women in the camp always helped each other. To make matters worse, I was put on a farriers' course away at Ambala. It lasted a month. On it were farriers from all the Cavalry Regiments, some Artillery men, Transport Corps, and even a Scotsman, a Seaforth Highlander, kilt and all. I enjoyed the course and came out with a Distinguished Pass, much to my delight, and my Regiment's. I think my horse drawings had helped me a lot.

The year had started very well for us, but things changed when Evie was near to having the baby. "Complications," they said. The baby arrived, a girl, on 18th September 1928, and died the same day. Sadness and devastation are the words that come to mind. Evie and I named her Patricia Charmaine. I do hope she still lies in eternal peace in Risalpur.

Just after our family problem, we had another. The Regiment had to return to England. As Evie was not fully recovered from our loss, I decided we would stay in India and I would transfer to the 4/7 Dragoon Guards instead of moving all the way back to the UK. I also knew Evie didn't want to move back just yet. She said there was still a lot more of India she wanted to see.

# PAGE 59

We said goodbye to the Regiment and friends I had known for years. It was a very hard thing to do. Then Evie and I started a new life with a new Regiment, my third. So it was 'hello Sialkot' and 'hello 4/7 Dragoon Guards'. We both settled in very well, and still enjoyed our life together in India.

If the opportunity came around, we would travel to different parts of India enjoying the best we could. Evie liked riding around the Murree Hills, as it was much cooler and more bearable. In 1929 the 4/7th Dragoon Guards got notice to move back to the UK, and this time Evie and I could not get out of it. So we ended back in the UK, me, after seven years away.

We were stationed at Shorncliffe Barracks in Kent. We took over the horses from the 13/18 Hussars then got on with our training. We had some good news. Evie was due to have another baby in May. To our delight, our Raymond was born on 15th May 1930, and all was well for both baby and Evie. As soon as word got around, different ones of our families came down to see us.

## PAGE 60

We had just under two years at Shorncliffe Barracks. Then we all moved again to Aliwal Barracks, Tidworth, Hampshire, by Salisbury Plain. It was a good camp that we took over from the Queen's Bays. As usual everyone got stuck into their work. Some nights we would go out rabbit hunting with .22 rifles and a couple of cars, then we would catch the rabbits in the car lights, which seemed to mesmerise them long enough for us to shoot them. There was always plenty of rabbit stew on families' tables.

There was a big worry about the Cavalry Regiments losing their horses for tanks, cars and lorries. It was a very hard pill to swallow. In 1934 the 3rd Hussars moved into the next Barracks to us. They were the first Cavalry mob to get mechanised into tanks. They were a great bunch of lads, but they were not happy about losing their horses. However, it didn't deter them in their task ahead. Some of their farrier staff came to our Mess, then they would come back to our quarter, and Evie would have a big pot of curry on the stove for them, which everyone enjoyed except me. It's funny, after nearly ten years in India, I didn't like the stuff.

## PAGE 61

In October 1935 Evie had another son, Derek. He was only a month old when we all had to move again, this time to Edinburgh, Scotland. Our Raymond went on ahead with a very good mate of mine, 'Seedy Cake'. He had been transferred from the 3rd Hussars, with promotion. So he and his wife, Beauty, looked after Raymond until Evie, Derek and I arrived at Redford Barracks, to take over another quarter. As is normal in the Army, we all settled in pretty quickly. Lieutenant Aizlewood had by now become Colonel of the Regiment. I met him at Catterick some 47 years later and, believe it or not, he had driven all the way up from Cornwall in his slippers! A nice man.

So many of us went to London for King George VI's coronation. As a farrier my job was to see that all the horses we took were in tip-top condition for the parade. With us were Major Mullens, Lieutenant d'Avigdor-Goldsmid, Lieutenant J Leigh and RSM Townsend. It was a great occasion to be on.

As the years were passing, my two boys were growing up and making problems. Firstly, Raymond got knocked down by a truck after not looking, when getting off a tram. Luckily for him it was a very hot day. The tar on the road was soft, and they said it had saved him from being more seriously injured. To this day, he still has a little black mark under his nose.

# PAGE 62

The family had many good outings to Portobello, a local seaside resort. We had some really good times there. Some of our families would also come with us.

We had a few more upsets, with our Derek not being as angelic as he looked. He flooded the camp tennis courts not long before a tennis tournament was to be played. Another time he and a friend pulled all the heads off a Regimental flower display. And again, when on parade, they found little finger-prints on my sword it meant big trouble for me.

In 1938 we came to the worst, having to part with our horses.

The 4/7 Dragoon Guards last horse parade was at Dreghorn Loan, an open area near Redford Barracks. Two hundred mounted ranks in service dress, with swords drawn, formed up in review order opposite the saluting base. It was a sad time for everyone. The drum horse, 'Jubilee', a skewbald, stood there with silver drums shining as the Regiment's horses marched off for the last time in more than 250 years. The stables were now empty. That was the signal for myself to leave the Army after almost twenty years. I could not face having no more horses. What else could a Farrier Sergeant do?

# PAGE 63

## 1ˢᵗ TROOP, A SQUADRON, 5ᵗʰ ROYAL IRISH LANCERS
## N W F P Risalpur, India, 1920

Officer:     Lieutenant ?

NCOs        Sergeant Jock Anderson, Sergeant Cotton, Corporal Hennery, Lance Corporal Cronk.

Troopers:   Kerridge, O'Toole, Brown, Chaney, Turner, Hatton, Meakin, Oleson, Wilde, Denning, Stapleton, Higgs, Eccleton, Ralph, Mitchell.

### INDIAN NAMES AND NUMBERS

| | | |
|---|---|---|
| ECK = 1 | Budgie = time | Connah = food |
| DOH = 2 | Jow = go | Mergy = chicken |
| TEEN = 3 | Innerow = come | Metre = toilets |
| CHAR = 4 | Jildy = hurry | Coggage = paper |
| PONCH = 5 | Asty = slow | Pice = money |
| CHAY = 6 | Wappus = turn about | Dude = milk |
| SART = 7 | Buss = stop | Cheeny = sugar |
| ART = 8 | Gummow = turn | Char = tea |
| NOO = 9 | Turie = knife | Muccin = butter |
| DUS = 10 | Contah = fork | Routy = bread |
| GARA = 11 | Cummage = spoon | Unders = eggs |
| BARA = 12 | Bundukh = rifle | |

I also remembered seventy-two more names of 5ᵗʰ Lancers, but I thought I should mention my good mate, Walter Critchley, who travelled with me to Salisbury when we joined up. He was a saddler in the Regiment and when we all split up I went to the 'Skinns' and he went to the 4ᵗʰ Hussars.

## 1st TROOP HQ SQUADRON 5th INNISKILLING DRAGOON GUARDS

Officer: Lieutenant ?

NCOs  Sergeant White, Farrier Corporal Meakin, Corporal Andrews, Lance Corporal Renvoise.

Troopers: Gutteridge, Tyas, McDonnah, Fryer, Fisher, Hodgson, Davis, Ginger Jones, Musgrove, Lawler, Whittaker, Wilkins, Harris, Whitehead, Darky Murrey, Farrier Clarke.

# PAGE 64

Civvy Street was a complete stranger to me and my family. We moved from Edinburgh back home (for me, that is). We moved in with my parents in Trevor Road, Orrell Park, still in the Walton area. I know Evie was not too keen on living with my parents, but that was to be expected. Still, we were not there all the time. We also visited her mother in York for a while.

In 1939 I found a job at Gilmores. They were hauliers and had twenty heavy horses which I could look after as a farrier. I settled into it quickly and just loved working with these great animals.

In the meantime we had found a house in Maghull, just outside Liverpool. Evie really liked the place. We even had a stream at the bottom of the garden. But I'm afraid we did not stay there too long. As war had broken out again, the travelling for me to and from work on a bicycle was hair-raising at times. It was a total of about sixteen miles a day. So we all moved into Liverpool to be closer to work. Evie found a nice house with garden at 69 Morval Crescent, Walton, a good area, until the bombing started.

# PAGE 65

Gilmore's, where I worked, was near the dock road and we had some heavy bombing attacks. When I reached work one morning there was nothing left – no buildings – no stables – and worst of all, no horses – only bits of them hanging about the ruins. I just broke down and cried.

It all started on 25th June 1940 and by 25th September there had been 121 air raids on the City. Most of our evenings were spent in the air raid shelter in the garden.

We had a railway line nearby and it was the line they used to move cargoes from the docks, so the German planes attacked it. People at the end of the street were all killed by a direct hit one night. A friend of Derek's took him to see the cannon shell holes in his bedroom; and us, and most of our neighbours lost our windows. Most places had lost their windows, especially the shops, but there was one lucky butcher who hadn't. He put up a sign saying "BECAUSE OF HITLER THE PORTIONS ARE LITTLER". Very fitting!

As things were felt to be getting worse, I decided to pack Evie and the boys off to York to her mother. I thought it was safer for them there.

## PAGE 66

Evie and the boys travelled by train from Lime Street Station to York. All the way they were attacked by German planes. They had to change trains at Leeds. Whilst waiting for their connection a mine was dropped just outside the station. The explosion blew them all off their feet. Evie and Derek went one way while Raymond ended up across the tracks onto the opposite platform. Evie and Derek had no suitcases, just the handles. Thank goodness they were only badly shaken. On the next train a train-driver going off duty handed Evie a cup of cold tea to steady her down. They were all glad to get to Grandma's house.

I had now got a job at Rollo's Ship Repairers as a blacksmith. I was working there until I was made redundant in 1959. The City was still being heavily bombed when I started. The Cathedral was damaged and the City centre was flattened, but the docks got the worst hits.

There were three very big explosions. An ammunition ship blew up. The Bootle Match works blew up, and an ammunition train blew up near Broadway. They were very bad times. I thought 'Thank goodness my family was out of it for now.'

On 17th October the Fazakerley Sanatorium was flattened. On 23rd October Liverpool had its 200th air raid. In December a fire engine responding to a call in Roe Street disappeared into a crater, killing all the crew. I also had a few scary times just travelling to and from work.

## PAGE 67

After eighteen months away Evie, Raymond and Derek came home to Morval Crescent, much to my delight. I told the boys that while they were away their school had just missed getting blown up. What happened was that a mine came down by parachute and blew up three streets: Arnot Street, Index Street and Lowell Street. Arnot Street was where the boys school was, but apart from losing its windows, it survived much to the disappointment of the local school kids.

A little later, in 1943, we had a very exciting time. This also included a mine. It came down and knocked the corner of a house down, which belonged to a mate of the boys. Luckily it didn't go off, or I wouldn't be writing this. Colin's mother came downstairs into the kitchen and almost stood on the mine. She was in terrible shock when she found out what it was.

The next morning, quite early, the police moved all the residents from their homes. Everyone was moved to the scout hut building in Walton Village. The family had to stay there for two days so that the mine could be made safe. Rollo's, where I worked was also hit but, lucky for me, not the smithy where I worked so it didn't stop me from working.

## PAGE 68

In Liverpool they had a German Messerschmitt fighter plane by St. George's Hall. I think half of the population went to see it. I took the boys to see it. You could see people wanted to tear pieces off it, but the police kept them off. Most of the kids then had tins or jars with shrapnel in them, collected from bombed houses, and around the streets.

The allied troops were now in Italy, and things had just started to quieten down. We didn't need our air raid shelter as much. But it was still not easy. The rationing was very tight. There were queues, long ones, all over. It was very hard for the wives, especially over Christmas, and the cold weather was no help. All we could do was our best. Thank goodness I had plenty of work. There were always plenty of ships to repair in those days. During 1944 life improved, especially with the War news. June 6th saw our lads attacking Europe and so on. We even managed to get a few oranges, which Derek had never seen before.

The Winter was a very cold one, but as a family we knew we could put up with it after the past problems. When it all ended there were victory parties all over. Liverpool went mad. Everyone had flags out, and we had a big party for the children of Morval Crescent.

*My Father wrote these pages in York after my Mother died in 1980. He decided to visit friends in New Zealand, for six months so he did not write any more completely. He just made a short list of what he intended to do. I have deciphered them as best as I could and have presented them in his style of writing. (Derek Meakin)*

## PAGE 69

1946 was a special year for Evie and me because Raymond decided to join the Army, as I did long ago. Ray had a job in a printer's which was very good those days, but his feet were itchy for travelling. I was very proud of him because he completed 42 years, and ended up as a Major.

There was plenty of work for me and many others in the ship repair industry.

In 1948 I became Treasurer for the 'Penny in the Pound' at Rollo's.

With Raymond not at home now, we had a spare room, so we got a lodger to help out with the money. He was Mr. Rollinson. He worked in the offices of Richmond Sausage Company in Litherland. He only stayed about nine months.

In 1949 Raymond came home on leave before a posting to Egypt. Like father, like son. So before he went abroad Ray, Derek and I went on a cycling holiday to the Norfolk Broads and a good time was had by all. I was still getting on with my job.

# PAGE 70

In 1950 I was made Union Treasurer, so I had to step down from my 'Penny in the Pound' job as it was too much to contend with.

Derek left school this year and started work at Sayers as an apprentice confectioner. He enjoyed it there and quite a few of his workmates came out with us on bicycles. They were a great bunch of lads. We all enjoyed our Sunday rides out. We would all gather at the Pier Head to get the ferry across the Mersey and go to places like Chester, Wrexham, Rhyl, Conway and Bala. One of our best rides was to Llangollen then over the Horseshoe Pass, across the Llandegla Moor, into Mold, Chester, then back to Liverpool. It kept us all busy. It wasn't just Wales we visited, we cycled to Blackpool, Buxton, the Lake District, my Mother's at Sedbergh, and many more places, but not all in one year.

1952 brought a new change again, for we had another lodger, a Mr. Ted Myres. He had also worked with Shire horses at Crosby Council, but as the poor horses were being phased out he'd ended up at Sayers, in the Stores. Yes, the same place that Derek worked. We all got about together for holidays, over the years, to Torquay, Ilfracombe, and Greenodd near Lake Coniston.

# PAGE 71

1955 was Derek's last holiday before being called up for his National Service. So in May, he and I cycled up to Edinburgh. We got attacked by black-headed seagulls while cycling near Selkirk.

Derek joined the 3$^{rd}$ Hussars in tanks. It was a Regiment I was very familiar with. He was in it for two years, then the Territorial Army for six more. All the while that Derek was away his girl-friend, Ann, spent a lot of time at our house, which we were very happy about.

In 1956 I went cycling around Southern Ireland, with Ronnie Ainsworth, one of our Derek's mates from Sayers Bakery. We had an unforgettable time over there.

Derek was demobbed in 1957 and started back to work at Sayers. He married Ann on 3$^{rd}$ July, 1958.

Evie, Ted and I had another holiday in the Lake District. We loved it up there.

In 1959 I was made redundant from Rollo's after seventeen years' service. It was quite a blow for me, but we did get some good news that year, when Ann and Derek gave us a grandson, Billy.

I was not out of work too long and started again at Top Mast, still helping to repair ships. I stayed for about a year then found another job at Howsons. The work was a bit heavier though. It entailed repairing anchor chains, and climbing masts. My biggest job was climbing the Mammoth. That was, at that time, the largest floating crane in the world. I'd always told Evie I couldn't clean her windows because I didn't like heights, so I was in trouble when the Liverpool Echo put a photo of me in the paper, on top of this crane.

# PAGE 72

I was at work around the docks visiting different ships, doing jobs for Howsons up to when I was sixty-five, when I expected to get retired. But they asked me to stay on as they were pleased with my work, so I did until 1968, when Evie was not too well. I packed it in to look after her full-time. By that time Ann and Derek had three sons, Bill, Alan and Howard; and in August 1968 Ann had a little girl, Carol. They were all such lovely children.

By 1971 Evie was a lot worse. I'm afraid the cigarettes were catching up with her. I bought a wheelchair so we could get out for short walks, and even had the odd holiday. All this time Ted was still living with us, since 1952, but he died of Leukaemia in 1975. He was buried at Litherland cemetery. We had always shared jobs about the house, so I found I had a little more to do now, as well as looking after Evie.

It got to the point that Evie was in bed more than out of it. The doctor was a very regular visitor to Morval Crescent. She died in bed on 2$^{nd}$ April, 1979, after fifty-nine years of marriage.

As she had wished, Raymond, Derek and I scattered her ashes by the Bar Walls in York, opposite the railway station. It was very hard for me when I gave her wheelchair away.

## PAGE 73

In June 1979 Derek moved up to York, on his own at first. He was to start a new job there with the MOD. Raymond was already living in York. So after forty years at Morval Crescent I moved away to York to be near my sons. I moved to Wenlock Terrace to a flat in a building that was a soldiers' home since 1909. Derek also lived in the same building, which was handy for me. It was good to be back where the old cavalry barracks used to be. It was 1922 since I was in the same area.

In November I went on a six months' break to New Zealand to stay with some friends in the North Island, a town called Whangarei, and I had a fantastic time. I was there for Christmas, which we all enjoyed on the beach. I also had a great 80th birthday party with my NZ friends and neighbours. It was an unforgettable and wonderful time. I got back to York on 13th May. It was hard settling in again.

I had started drawing and painting again. I had a lot of sketches from New Zealand so I started to improve on them. That's when I went to art school evening classes. They were very helpful to me and I enjoyed them very much.

The next couple of Winters were not to my liking, especially 1982. Firstly, snow, then freezing weather, and floods when things started to melt. It was very hard to get about with all the flooding, so I did not venture very far. There was talk of our soldiers' homes being sold off. Derek and Ann were offered a Council house in Tang Hall, not too far away, and I got the chance to move to Acomb at the other side of the river, in a Council flat. It was not great, but it saved me worrying too much. I felt New Zealand calling me again, so I went for my second six-month trip in 1983-4.

## PAGE 74

On my first trip to New Zealand, when coming home, I got friendly with two young New Zealanders. They were going to tour Europe in a camper van, just like many before them, so when they eventually reached York they stayed with me at Wenlock Terrace for a week. When they found out I was going over there again I got an invitation from their family to stay for a while at Christchurch, down in the South Island, which I accepted so I stayed with them at one stage during my six months in New Zealand. How lucky can one be to get a chance to visit so much of such a beautiful country?

When I got back home Derek and Ann were a little further away than before. At one stage I took ill with Shingles, right across my back. Derek used to cycle right across York to keep his eye on me. It lasted a few weeks and was very painful.

*My father took ill very quickly and we were not happy about him being alone across the City, so with a lot of persuasion we got him to move in with our Aunty Joyce. She lived at 8th Avenue in York, which was not far from my house. A little while later we found out that Dad had cancer of the lymph glands. Joyce gave him first class love and attention but he slowly got worse, so was moved into St. Leonard's Hospice. It was a fantastic place. As it was a new building he gave them some of his paintings for the walls. At one point he went to a Leeds hospital for therapy but he couldn't get back to York fast enough. When the hospice was officially opened by the Duchess of Kent she especially had a good chat with him about his service in the 4/7 Royal Dragoon Guards, because she was the Regiment's Colonel In Chief. I know that my Dad was so pleased that such a lovely Lady came to see him. She even gave him a signed portrait of herself. I thank her for helping to make my father's last few days so memorable.*

*After being the longest survivor at York Hospice, Dad passed away in September 1985. My brother Raymond and I were there with him.*

QUIS SEPARABIT

# MEMBERS OF THE PRITCHARD FAMILY

Elizabeth Pritchard Licensee of the Britannia Inn and the Ship Inn, York

John Pritchard Licensee of the Leeds Arms, York

Charlotte Pritchard in the doorway of The Leeds Arms, with her son, William Pritchard

Doris and Fred Pritchard

Violet Pritchard married Henry Taylor

Evie and William Meakin with son

Janet married Peter Pigott

# A BYGONE ERA

## BY

## VIOLET TAYLOR

Violet Taylor (née Pritchard) aged 21

# INTRODUCTION

After my Dad, Harry Taylor, died in 1992 my determined Mum chose to live an independent life in her own home in York for the next eight years. One weekend when I was staying with her she made a pot of tea, but spilt boiling water on her work surface and down her cupboard door. I realised that the time had come when it was dangerous for her to live on her own and persuaded her to come back with me to my home in the Midlands. A week later she collapsed and was admitted to my local hospital. When she recovered she asked me to find her a residential home in the area and never returned to York.

For the next five years my brother and his wife visited her regularly, a friend from York came to see her from time to time and I spent a vast amount time with her, listening to her repeated tales, and taking her for days out and appointments. Mum remembered her early life with absolute clarity. Despite my putting her yarns into sequence, and typing them for her, this is Mum's own story, not mine. Dates have been verified by her son-in-law, Peter Pigott, a Family History Researcher.

# A BYGONE ERA
# by
# Violet Taylor 1906 – 2006

## PARENTS

My Dad, John Pritchard, the only surviving son of Joseph and Elizabeth Pritchard who together ran The Britannia Inn in Walmgate, York in 1881, and later The Ship Inn in Skeldergate, was a great disappointment to his mother when he met and married my Mum, Charlotte Terrey, in 1893. Mum was a feisty, self-confident girl with a strong-willed personality, which his mother thought would dominate her son's life, but worst of all she was a Protestant.

Dad came from a large family of 10 children, 2 boys and 8 girls. Robert, the first son, born in September 1860 was lost at sea in 1879 but for whatever reason, he was never talked about. Apart from his older sister, Emma, I don't think any of his other sisters even knew about him. All the children were brought up in the Catholic faith by their devout Roman Catholic parents.

After my Dad's father died in 1886, his mother took over his licence of the Ship Inn in Skeldergate and by all accounts she was an overbearing woman who ruled the establishment with a rod of iron. She was distraught when she found out about her son's friendship with a Protestant, and when they were courting created much friction by her objections. When she eventually realised that her son would not obey her, because he and Mum were both legal adults who could please themselves about being married, she demanded that they must bring up any children of their union in the Catholic faith. Mum said:

'No way! My children will choose their own religions when they are old enough to do so'.

Despite his mother's protests and her Priest's intervention and pleas for Mum to convert to Catholicism, Dad gave way to Mum's desire to be wed in the Church of England, and they were married in Holy

Trinity Church, Micklegate, York, on 22nd October 1893 when he was 24 and she was 22 years of age.

Years later my Mum's sister, my Aunt Harriet, told me there weren't many supporters at the ceremony. Mum's father, my Grandpa Terrey, had died in 1891 when he fell from his horse and trap whilst delivering bolts of cloth to a customer in the village of Copmanthorpe just outside York. As my Grandma Terrey couldn't read or write, Aunt Harriet signed the wedding certificate, along with Dad's Best Man, his friend, William Fentiman.

At the time of their marriage, Dad worked as a driller at the Railway's Carriage Works in York – and Mum was a tailoress. She had been apprenticed to her father, William Terrey, who was a Master Tailor by trade. She made all her own clothes, and those for my brother William and sister Evie.

After their marriage Dad and Mum and her sister Harriet lived with my Grandma Terrey at 49 Price Street near Nunnery Lane. My brother, William (Billie), was born there on 30th January 1897 and another brother, Sydney, was born in June 1901 but unfortunately the baby didn't survive beyond a few weeks. It was a great sadness to my parents, and they didn't have another child until Evie was born in 1903.

With a growing family, more money was needed and when the Engineering Section in which Dad worked was moved from York to The Locomotive Works at North Road Shops in Darlington, Dad went with them as a painter, which was promotion for him because he got more money.

I was born in Darlington on 1st December 1906 at 26 Gurney Street.

## OUR PUBLIC HOUSE

When I was about a year old Dad moved back to York. The reason for this was because he was a great sportsman. He loved playing rugby football and at one of the matches he'd had his back kicked which led to serious spinal injuries in later years. After the accident he couldn't do his job as efficiently as before, and he was permanently in a lot of pain.

The Pritchard family in York was a large one and by that time nearly all of them ran public houses. So when Dad heard about Bentley's Breweries wanting a licensee for The Leeds Arms in Peaseholme Green he went after the job and got it. After he moved back to York with his family, another two children were born: Doris in 1909 and Fred in 1911.

The pub was situated on the corner of Peaseholme Green and Haymarket. It had six bedrooms but no bathroom. In the yard outside we had a zinc bath which Mum used to bring into the kitchen and we had a 6-foot high 3-sided screen which she put round the bath to hide our modesty. She filled buckets of water from a pump in the yard, then carried them through to the kitchen and heated the water in a boiler which had a brass tap on it. The boiler was situated at the side of the fireplace, and we also had pans and kettles on the fire to top up the water when it got cooler. Emptying the bath when we'd finished was a time-consuming job for her so we children only used to have a bath once a week, one after the other.

In addition to the six bedrooms upstairs there was an enormous, huge room. It went over the entrance passage where you came in, right over the Bar, Snug and Smoke Room; and over the kitchen the other way. There was a big fireplace in it. There were two windows. One looked onto Peaseholme Green and the other onto Haymarket. Mum put beautiful curtains up. She always had lovely lace curtains.

As children, we used to go and play in the big room, but once a month Dad used to let a Society that he belonged to use it as a meeting room. He never charged them for the use of it, he just loaned it to them. I'm not sure, but I think it was called the Society of Buffaloes, and I think they were based in St. Saviourgate.

Our pub was next door to the Black Swan public house where Dick Turpin is said to have stayed. There was also another pub at the other side of the street, The Woolpack. But we had no shortage of customers. We used to get a lot of courting couples come – they came for years – it was a good meeting place for them. They used to congregate in our Lounge where the seating was very nice. It was all mahogany up the backs, and had lovely leather seats. Sometimes the room was so full, couples had to stand. We also had our regulars in the Bar and Smoke Room in addition to any passing trade.

There were stables in the yard outside where we housed our pony and trap and Mum and Dad rented a couple of stables out to local farmers.

We didn't have television in those days, so some of the chaps used to come forward and play the piano and sing for entertainment and people would join in and sing the songs of the day such as Burlington Bertie and The Old Bull and Bush. Our Billie soon picked them up and taught himself to play by ear. He only had to hear a song once, and was able to play it. Even as a young boy he used to be piano-crazy. He'd twiddle his fingers on the tablecloth and say he was playing the piano. He turned out to be a really excellent pianist.

## SCHOOLDAYS

My schooldays in York were happy. Our Evie and I used to walk from Peaseholme Green, past St. Saviourgate, up High Ousegate and Micklegate where we stopped and knocked on the door of a large house to collect one of our friends, then we walked up to Priory Street where the school was situated in two parts. Girls on one side. Boys on the other.

My lessons were interesting. I can remember the Headmaster and two of the teachers, but I can't remember their names.

One teacher used to do Homecraft lessons and every now and again we used to have to take ingredients and cook or bake something. I remember having to make a cake. Mum weighed out the things I needed and put them in a basket. When the cakes were cooking mine didn't rise. It looked as flat as a pancake. So I cooked it longer than I should have done in the hope that it would come up more. But it didn't. With leaving it longer it went almost black and was as hard as iron. When it was time to go home and our Evie saw it she laughed like a drain. I'd forgotten to put any baking powder in it. Evie was always a bit of a mischief and she jibed and goaded me. She said:

'You can't take that thing home to our Mum, who's such a brilliant cook. She'll have a fit!'

So we took it out of the basket and bouled it all the way down Micklegate hill, patting it with our hands, whooping, and chasing after it like madmen. Bits flew off it and eventually there was nothing left to take home. When Mum asked what had happened to the cake that she was going to give to us for our tea, she was sharp-tongued about the cost of the ingredients but said it was a lesson I would always remember; and I have.

Nowadays there's such a thing as self-raising flour, but old habits die hard and I still prefer to use plain flour for cakes and carefully fold in the baking powder at the end. Done that way they always seem to come up lighter. And I've never ever forgotten to put baking powder in again.

Dad's injuries got worse and eventually he became bed-ridden with paralysis of the spine. Mum made us older ones help with some of the chores, young as we were, much to Evie's dislike. I was only 10 when Dad started to be really immobile, but I helped with cleaning, dusting, setting the table, and making sandwiches. Sometimes I even helped in clearing out the spittoons. Our Doris and Fred were too young to help in the pub. Doris was three years younger than me and Fred hadn't started school then.

During that time Castlegate School was being built at the back of Craven's sweet factory in Coppergate. It backed onto Piccadilly. It was much closer to Peaseholme Green. So when it was finished, our Doris went there.

The Council took over Priory Street School which had previously been a private school and Mum had paid sixpence each per term for us to go there. That's 2½p by today's prices. So after that I went to Castlegate school as well as Doris, and eventually our Fred went there as well. Our Evie didn't have long before she was due to finish, but she moved there for a short while. When she left, she refused to work in the pub and went to work in the Cardboard Box Department at Rowntree's chocolate factory. They used to make large specialist boxes of chocolates, and Evie loved the job. She was very happy there and made lots of friends.

Mum was so busy serving in the pub at nights she never knew, but after Evie left school, she used to slope off and go out dancing nearly every night. The Grand Picture House in Clarence Street had a ballroom over it, so she only had to go over Lord Mayor's Walk to reach it. When she was 17 she met her future husband, Billy Meakin, there.

Doris and Fred were very clever children. Our Doris was good at English and Fred excelled at arithmetic. I was also good at arithmetic. I used to have to add up the price of beer in my head – it looked bad if I had to write it down on paper – so I learnt to tot up very quickly, and I made very few mistakes. I was also quite good at spelling, so I think the teachers at Priory Street School had taught us very well.

## WORKING IN THE PUB

Dad's paralysis got worse. He died when I was only 11 and after that I often had to take days off school to help Mum. I had to stand on an upturned beer crate to reach the pumps. On a couple of occasions the School Board Man came round to find out why I was missing, so I had to hide until he'd gone.

When I left school at 14 Mum couldn't wait for me to help her full-time. The wife of Jack Wragg, one of our regular customers was already engaged as a full time helper. Mum also had a couple of girls working part-time for her but they tended to be unreliable so she wanted to get rid of them and for me and Mrs Wragg to work together and look after things for her. I did that until I was 24 years of age. Then I got a job as a sales assistant at Marks & Spencer's.

I enjoyed my work at the pub. At first Mum paid me 5 shillings a week (25p by today's prices). Over the years she raised it to seven shillings and six pence a week, but she provided me with all my clothes, accommodation, food and expenses. That was just pocket-money, really. I knew all the regular customers and had many a good laugh with them.

One evening when I was working in the pub one of the customers, who had a large waxed moustache, asked me to bring him a light for his pipe. I lit a long taper from the coal fire and took it over to him. I was holding it up to give him when another customer attracted my attention. He called to me and asked me to fill up his glass. I turned to tell him that I'd get it in a minute, and heard George screaming. When I turned back, his moustache was on fire. Someone threw his drink over George's face to put the blaze out, but it was too late. Half his moustache had gone. Poor George! He had to shave the other half off. But he was a nice man and he forgave me. Perhaps I got away with it because I was so young! He did eventually grow another 'tache which was much bushier than the one before but he didn't wax it again.

Working in the pub was physically hard work and we all worked long hours. The sort of jobs we used to do were sweeping and scrubbing floors, mopping out the beer cellar, cleaning out spittoons every day, which contained the ashes of smokers' pipes and shag tobacco, and they had to be replaced with clean sawdust. Percy Fentham, a hired hand, washed glasses, cleared away empties and sorted them into their appropriate crates, swilled the yard outside, generally looked after the stables, and did odd jobs as required. Mrs Wragg cleaned and polished wooden tables, benches and our beautiful wooden-backed furniture which had leather seats, kept the place clean and tidy, and helped with the laundry. All of us children made our own beds and kept our bedrooms tidy.

As well as serving in the bar in the evenings, although Dad was the licensee, Mum managed the pub, as well as cooking all our meals, and looking after our family so well. When he'd been alive, Dad did a lot of this work until he was paralysed and became bed-ridden. Then the work he'd done had to be shared out amongst us, as delegated by Mum. Apart from playing the piano for entertainment in the pub, which he didn't get paid for, Billie never worked there. When he left school he went as an apprentice chemist to a firm in Bootham. But of course, all that changed when he went to the war.

After Dad died in 1918, my Uncle, Jack Varley, used to come from Darlington once a fortnight and helped by serving in the pub over the weekend. Sometimes he would bring his little daughter, Renee, and she would play with our Doris and Fred.

## PARTY TIMES

Christmases were usually nice times. Mum used to decorate the pub. We'd have a decorated tree and she'd make mince pies and put out a big dishful on Christmas Eve and customers would help themselves. Our Billie would play carols and everyone would sing to them, but the biggest celebrations were always on New Year's Eve.

We had to have our parties after the pub closed, and Mum had to get special permission for us to remain open an hour extra on New Year's Eve and to have the lights on upstairs. So the pub would be open until 11 o'clock, and all the regulars that were in the pub that night were invited to join us.

Mum would make a great big buffet meal for us to come back to. She would do a whole ham and everything to go with it, and put it in the big pantry that we had in the kitchen. Percy would stay and a couple of women would also stay to help him. They laid the tables and had our suppers ready in the big room upstairs for when we got back. Everyone else would go down Aldwalk in a big gang, singing, and we would listen to the Minster bells peal in the New Year. It was lovely. Then we would all come back for our supper.

After everything had been cleared away we had dancing in that huge room until about 5 o'clock in the morning. We could get 24 people in 3 sets of Lancers dancing on the floor together, Billie would play the piano for them to dance to. Everyone else would sit around the edges of the room. We all used to have a jolly good time. But these special occasions were few and far between in the years before the First World War started. As children, we used to have our birthday parties in the big room, but we didn't have them after hours like we did at New Year.

## THE FIRST WORLD WAR

When World War I broke out in August 1914 our Billie was 17 – 18 the following January. At first he was sent to Curragh Camp which was a basic training camp in Ireland. He was in the Army Ordnance Corps and while he was still 17 he was posted to France. Because the Ordnance Corps weren't so much involved in front-line action as some of the other troops, he used to entertain the soldiers in an Army hut on a night. Because he could sing and play the piano so well, the Head of the Battalion was taken up with his artistry and encouraged him to join the Army concert party, which he did. I don't know much about it because I wasn't there, I only know what I was told about it afterwards.

Fortunately we didn't get much war damage where we lived. No-one was killed inside the pub, but one man was killed outside it. At the front of the pub there was a passage that led into the lounge. At the front of the passage there was a wall bracket with a gas lamp on it. One night when a chap was putting the lamp out a bomb went off nearby and he was killed.

One night when I was about 9 or 10 years old, there was a zeppelin attack after we'd been put to bed. We had thick blackout curtains up at our windows, but there must have been a light showing at Hustwick's Lodging House in St. Saviourgate because eight or nine men were killed there when a bomb went off and part of the house was demolished. We were roused from our beds and taken down to the cellar. The wardens weren't as keen on checking that all the blackouts were drawn in the First World War as they were in the Second one.

We had two cellars – a very deep one downstairs where the beer barrels were kept – and a shallower one upstairs in the kitchen. Mum preferred to use the one in the kitchen because it was very handy for storing things for use in the pub. The cellars weren't damp. They had stone floors. We all had to sit in the kitchen cellar and wait quietly until it was safe to go back to bed again.

## DAD'S DEPARTURE FROM LIFE ON EARTH

While Billie was in France my Dad became seriously ill with his paralysis. Our Brewery was Bentley's Yorkshire Breweries of Leeds. They had a Manager that did all the business deals, like coming out to collect the cash, and taking the orders and so on. There were only two pubs in York that they supplied. The other wasn't really a pub, it was more like a bar, but it was run by Walter Todd and his place was in Davygate. Well, he became Lord Mayor, so on Mum's behalf this Brewery Manager asked him if he could get compassionate leave for our Billie to come over to see his Dad, and he got it for him. Billie came over for a fortnight – but he had to go back – and he hadn't been back long when Dad had another relapse and died in February 1918. This time they wouldn't allow Billie to come back again. So he never saw his Dad any more.

Dad had a big funeral. The service wasn't in the Catholic Church, but Mum did allow him to have the Last Rites, and a Catholic Priest conducted a service at the graveside after a traditional Church service; but that was as far as she would go so far as Catholicism was concerned. She had a caterer in at the pub and after the internment everyone came back to a proper sit-down meal in the big room upstairs. The caterers only provided the food, they didn't provide the drinks, so my Aunt Emma went to Percy Fentham and George Brown who worked in the Pub at that time and told them to see that everyone at the funeral had a drink on her and that she would pay the bill. Dad had been very well liked in his lifetime.

## PREPARING FOR BILLIE TO COME HOME FROM WAR

We had stables in our yard two of which were rented out to local farmers. One person who rented one of them wasn't a farmer, he was a cab-man who drove horses. This Mr. Calvert decided that as the war was coming to an end, he was going to have a pig and fatten it up for Christmas, to celebrate. Mum thought that was a good idea because things were a bit sticky as far as provisions were concerned, and she decided to have one as well. She insisted that they kept their pigs separately. He had his pig in one stable, she had hers in another.

When the time came to slaughter the pigs she approached Mr Webster, a butcher in Layerthorpe. He wanted to take both pigs to his slaughterhouse. But she refused to allow him to take hers. She wanted our pig to be killed in our own stable so that she was certain we were getting the right one and not Mr Calvert's by mistake. Mr Webster said it would not be hygienic to do it in our stable but she insisted. He equally insisted that the stable would have to be done out and the floor tarred to meet all the necessary standards. So she had the stable all done out properly and the pig was killed in our own stable.

When the deed was all done she had flitches of bacon hung up in our side passage, and all the stuff she didn't want, such as the liver, offal, bones, trotters and such, she put onto long dishes for customers in the pub to come and help themselves to feed their dogs. They thought their Christmas had come early! Some of the men told Mum afterwards that they'd actually eaten some of the offal themselves after their wives had cooked it, and their wives had stewed the bones and made broth, and they'd enjoyed it. I don't know what Mr Calvert did with his offal, but we never ate liver, kidneys, hearts, or so on, so the men were welcome to it.

Another thing Mum did in preparation for Billie coming home in August 1918, was to have the big room upstairs completely re-furnished. She said she was going to do it as a thanksgiving for his safe return.

Mum no longer loaned the room to the Society that Dad had lent it to free of charge and they had their meetings elsewhere. She had that huge room cleaned by Bellerbys Decorators, which had the best reputation in York, and they came in and thoroughly cleaned and re-decorated it. When they'd finished she went to Leake & Thorpe's and had a Wilton carpet made, because they didn't sell one big enough to fit the room. It was all greens and reds, and was beautiful. After it had been fitted all over the room she bought a sofa and seven matching easy chairs, and had them arranged all round the room. Then she bought a big walnut sideboard to go along the side wall, and a whatnot which she put ornaments on. Finally, she bought a piano of the highest quality. When our Billie saw it he was thrilled, and marvelled at where she'd got the money from to pay for it all.

Being a qualified tailoress when she was younger, she'd learnt how to cut her cloth wisely and not waste material, which cost money, and she had followed this procedure of thrift in running the pub. Because she'd been apprenticed to her father, as part of the trade, Grandpa Terrey had taught her how to keep the books and budget well. I suppose she'd saved some money in her lifetime, plus the fact that she had a little policy with

The Heart of Oaks Friendly Society which probably matured when Dad died. So it was all a very pleasant and unexpected surprise for Billie. They went to St. Cuthbert's Church, got on their knees, and thanked The Lord for looking after him during the war and bringing him safely home.

## AFTER THE WAR WAS OVER

Our Billie had a girl-friend before he went to the war. She was a year younger than him and her name was Jessie Winter but after the war things were very different. He found out she hadn't been faithful to him so he called the relationship off. Mum was quite upset about it, because Jessie had come to our house all through the war and we'd all got very friendly with her and her sisters Dolly and Eva. However, that was that, but I stayed friendly with her, and we were friends for years.

Also, Billie didn't want to go back to being trained as a chemist, so he gave that up as well. He turned to music in a big way. He decided he wanted to be able to play classical music such as Rachmaninov and so on. So he went to a very good piano teacher, Mr. Connell, who used to play organ music at one of the Churches in York. He had a very good reputation as a classical piano teacher and taught Billie well. It was a joy to listen to him practising on that lovely piano in the big room upstairs.

Instead of going back to train as a chemist, Billie set up a concert party called the Blue Chevrons. There were eight chaps in it; and he formed a Roadio Band of six men. Billy was on the piano, and he had a drummer, a violinist, a saxophonist, a chap on a clarinet, and one on a banjo. They went all over Yorkshire entertaining people – to Lord Feversham's at Helmsley – out to Escrick, and so on, but his favourite venue was at the Ebor Hall behind Leake & Thorpe's.

There was a yard that went down the side of the shop. At the bottom there was a door which led into a gorgeous ballroom. It had a beautiful floor to dance on. Sometimes on a Saturday night after I'd finished serving pints at ten o'clock, I'd leave Percy to clear up and help Mum, and I'd run like mad from Haymarket, into Coney Street via Spen Lane, across the market, down New Street and into that yard to spend the last couple of hours there dancing before it closed at midnight.

When concert bookings started to tail off, Billie heard of a full-time job on the front at Scarborough, selling sheet music for Marks & Spencer. Someone was wanted to sing the tunes, and someone else was wanted to play the music. But our Billie could do both, so he got the job. Eventually that led him into being a Manager of the music department. However, further management training took him to other stores and other management positions. One of the places he went to was Kettering, where he met his future wife, Gwen Wright, but he was 40 by the time he married her. They settled in Nottingham, and retired to Wales. They had a very clever son and daughter. Terry became a Designer and worked in the television and film industries and retired to live in Spain. Angela was a Domestic Science teacher who moved to live in Brussels after her marriage. She and her husband, Tony, were there for over 20 years. Now they're both retired, too, and currently live in Kent

## MY YOUNGER BROTHER

When Fred was at school he was a very clever boy. Always top of his class. He should have gone on, and used his brain, but he was just mad about cars and craved to work with them. He was only just turned 6 when Dad died in 1918. Mum was always busy running the pub, so she let him have his own way more than she should.

When he left school he went to be an apprentice motor mechanic at the Castle Garage in York. After he'd been there about 1½ years he back-chatted his boss, and got finished. So he had to look for another job.

At that time there was a wholesale grocery firm in North Street called Johnson, Dodds & Co. They sold provisions, and all sorts of things, and their staff used to go all over the county – and into little villages – selling their wares. They had a very good salesman who was their top man but he didn't like driving so they advertised for a driver to take this man about his business. Our Fred got the job.

They used to load the van up and go all over the place; except on Mondays. Mondays were always spent working in York.

One of the places they used to go to was Ripon and it was there that Fred first met Molly Oliver. She was a waitress in one of the cafés in the market place that they used to go to.

Eventually the salesman retired and the new man did his own driving so Fred found a salesman's round of his own – with Country Dairies Ltd. In those days it was like the Rington's Tea firm. They used to have rounds selling tea and other produce – and as Fred's round included going to Ripon he continued to see Molly.

In March 1940 Fred got called up to serve in the second world war, and went into the RAF. Mum made up a big parcel to send to him for Christmas that year. This included some items from Molly, because we were only allowed to send one parcel.

For almost a year that parcel followed him around. In the end it came back to us, and it was absolutely intact, just as Mum had sent it. She was distraught. She thought he was dead. Anyway, about a year and a half after that we were notified by the Air Ministry that Fred was in a hospital in Australia, but they didn't say which hospital or where so we still couldn't write to him.

When he came back two years later, he told us that he had been sent abroad, to work on a big airport at Keppel Harbour in Singapore – but we didn't know that at the time because we only had a BFPO number to write to. While he was out there the area had been very badly bombed and they had tried to get the men out on aeroplanes and in boats. Fred had been put on a boat but it got torpedoed and he was in the water for two whole days before he was rescued and he eventually ended up in Australia. After he returned to England he was given an early discharge.

He went to see Molly. She was still working as a waitress in the same café. They were married in York Registry Office in 1945. Mum didn't like her very much but she said:

'It's not up to us. He's gone through enough in this war. It's his choice. We must stand by him.'

After they got married Molly moved to York with him. They got a flat in Stonegate and she took on two jobs. In the evenings she used to work in the basement of Betty's Café Tea Rooms in St. Helen's Square. It was always full of service-men; soldiers, airmen and the like. And she also had a day job as a waitress at Borders in Coney Street.

They were married for quite a few years before they had a child. They had a lovely little girl that they named after my Mum: Charlotte.

After the war was over Fred tried for the Civil Service, passed the entrance exams, and got into the Air Ministry. He spent some time working in Persia and Aden and then worked at Shelley House in Acomb. While he was there, he got the job as clerk of works for the building of a new RAF airport at Gan, His experience in working on a military airport during the war, and his ability to cope with extremely hot weather must have helped with his application.

When the job was complete he returned to York and continued to work for the Civil Service until he retired.

## MY YOUNGER SISTER

Doris was a very clever girl at school. She wanted to go to school, and she wanted to achieve, which she did. After completing her education at Castlegate school she had the ambition to be a secretary and begged Mum to let her try for the Technical College exams. Mum liked achievers, so was delighted when Doris passed the exam, and encouraged her to do well. She learnt to do shorthand and typing and went to work in Rowntree's offices, where she had a very good job.

Doris was a very sporty person. She loved to cycle and swim, and whenever she could she used to go to Yearsley Baths in the summer, and St. George's baths in the winter. She became a Girl Guide and used to go camping with them. She attained lots of badges, and eventually became the Guide Captain for the Heslington Road Guide Company in York She was always full of fun, a great organiser and, like Billy, a great entertainer with her singing, dancing and concerts to raise funds for the Guides.

She met "Boy Watson", a young featherweight boxer, and they married in June 1933. They bought a lovely new semi-detached house in Lilac Avenue, up Hull Road, and were very happy there. Then, a decade later, tragedy struck when their lovely little boy, Geoffrey, died with rheumatic fever. Everyone in the family was devastated. We were all grief-stricken at his sad, sudden demise. Doris was heavily pregnant at the time and three weeks later gave birth to another boy whom she named Howard. She cared for him and loved him as she'd never loved before. For a long time she was still in shock, and it took her great courage to come to terms with their plight. She and Joss had chosen to become Methodists and went to St. George's Church in Melrosegate. She found some solace in her faith and the support she got from the congregation, and after a while she continued her Guiding pastimes.

After her third son, Christopher, had been born she allowed the boys a lot of personal freedom and was not very strict with them when they were over-boisterous. Joss taught them how to box, and defend themselves, and they grew up to be very handsome, capable citizens who did well for themselves – Howard as a games and geography schoolteacher – and Christopher as a stonemason with a prominent business in Barry, Wales.

Joss worked for Sturge's, the analytical chemistry department of Rowntree's chocolate factory and each year they used to take the boys to Butlin's Holiday Camp at holiday times. One year they met Denis, Cath, and their daughter Denise, and through that friendship, were persuaded to leave Methodism and join the Christian Science religion.

When Doris had to go into hospital when the children were young, I had them at my house whilst Joss was at work. Whilst they were with me they both developed whooping cough. Dr. McKenzie, my Doctor, prescribed medicine to treat their symptoms. When Doris came out of hospital and saw the medicine she was horrified. She poured the remainder of it down the sink. Then I was horrified! We had a terrible row, and she took the children home. After that our personal relationships were never the same again. Apparently she believed that medicine had done nothing to save her first son, and God, and God alone, could make people better. We each kept to our own viewpoints, and it was many years before she abandoned Christian Scientism and returned to being a Methodist again.

## AFTER MUM'S RETIREMENT

When trade at the pub started to dwindle in the late 1930's, Mum decided to give up the licence and retire. She had already bought a terraced house in Scott Street in preparation for her retirement and had leased it to a couple of friends who knew she wanted it back eventually, so there wasn't a problem in getting her house back, and I moved in and lived with her there.

I had met a young chap, Harry Taylor, at a dance above the Regent Cinema when he had come to York to find work. He was a grocer by trade and as George Mason's had closed down in the Depression, he was looking for position as a Manager of another grocery shop. I was introduced to him by our Billie and his wife, Gwen.

At first I didn't like Harry very much, mainly because he was several years younger than me. However, we met by chance two or three times, and each time I liked him a little better than the last and eventually agreed to go out with him. Mum didn't think anything would come of the relationship because his home town was Gateshead in Northumberland, and mine was in York.

In 1936 he invited me to go to Gateshead for Christmas and meet his parents and sister. I decided I would to go, but Mum thought I would miss our large family gathering. Perhaps I would; but I went, mainly to see what sort of a home he came from. I must admit I found it very strange, and very quiet – just the four of them – when we were used to having such a lot of people around our Christmas table.

When Harry introduced me, his Dad and sister were lovely and warmly welcomed me to their home. But his mother's attitude was frosty. I got the impression that she took a dislike to me because I was a publican's daughter and she didn't think I was good enough for him; plus the fact that she thought I was too old for him.

My hackles rose. I suddenly realised what it must have been like for my Mum when Dad's mother had raised objections to their relationship. I was drawn closer to Harry in my indignity. I took a leaf out of my Mum's book and stood up for myself and my rights. We were married in St. Clement's Church, York on 18th April 1938.

My Mum was absolutely wonderful. She paid for everything. She gave me the glorious wedding that she'd never had. Harry's parents came and were very nice. His mother had got over her coolness towards me and his sister, Maisie, was a bridesmaid along with our Doris. My nephew, Geoffrey, was alive at that time, so he was a little page-boy.

Mum made my dress. It was in a white delicate fabric – georgette and taffeta – and I carried a bouquet of cream-coloured tea-roses. Mum also made Geoffrey's page-boy outfit in white satin, and my two bridesmaids wore satin dresses. They carried bouquets of blue irises to match the colour of their dresses.

Mum also paid for our reception at the Abbey Hotel on The Mount, and the photographs were taken by Taylor's of Micklegate. It was a wonderful occasion and I was married to Harry for 54 years, before he died from a heart attack on 7th July 1992.

We didn't have a honeymoon. Harry had the chance of managing the grocery section of a lock-up shop near the docks in Hull with me in charge of the beer-off section because of my experience of working in the pub. But he was the overall Manager. So we went straight to Hull. We rented a house in Graham Avenue, where you, Janet, were born the following year. As you know, your brother, Keith, was born in 1943, and you are both successful, enterprising people with good marriages yourselves.

Now I'm in my nineties I'm the only one left of my Mum's lovely family. All the rest have gone. You can remember what happened in your lifetime, and take over the story from me if you want to. I don't want to start thinking about the Second World War. I'd like to leave it at that.

These days there are times when I can't even remember what I had for breakfast this morning, or where I put the book down that I was reading a few minutes ago, yet I can remember as clear as a bell those things that happened so many years ago. I can visualise people's faces, and remember some of the things they said and did, just as if it was yesterday.

I hope I'll live to be 100. I won't get a telegram from the King because he died in the 1950's, but I might get a birthday card from his daughter, Queen Elizabeth 2nd. I hope I do. That would be very nice. I didn't like her mother – she posed far too much – and was a very strong-willed woman. But I like the Queen. She's nice! And I like the Duchess of Kent. She came to see Billy Meakin just before he died. It gave him a huge boost at the time, but unfortunately it didn't last too long. He died soon after that. Sometimes I think I've lived too long. Other times I think it would be a great achievement to be 100. What will be will be. We'll just have to wait and see."

*Violet had a stroke in December 2005 and died in January 2006, her centenary year, so her final ambition to reach her 100th birthday did not materialise. But she lived a long and happy life and her memories live on in the tales she told to anyone who was willing to listen to them. She gave me my life, loved, nurtured and guided me. I shall remember her for ever.*

# CROSSING THE CLASS DIVIDE?

# THE ENIGMA OF MARGARET WILSON BROWN

## BY

## MIKE RACE

Mike Race

# INTRODUCTION

Sometimes in our lifetime things happen unexpectedly. This story has been included because of a chance remark made during a telephone call.

I knew that Mike had been researching various members of his family for many years but I didn't know that he had written a story about his aunt, Margaret Race, who descended from the 5th of the Pritchard girls, Mary Ann (nicknamed Polly).

I said "What a pity I didn't know about this sooner, it could have gone into my book of Ancestral Tales, which I am preparing for publication." He replied "You can include it if you want to." I did want to. When I read it I found it to be a fascinating story and the amount of time Mike has spent on oral and family history deserves an accolade, especially his contributions to York Oral History Society over very many years.

Although I went to Bishopthorpe village almost every week from 1957-61 when I was serving as a Lieutenant, then Captain of the Girl Guide Company there, I never met Mike's Aunt, but I knew about her from my mother who was impressed by Margaret's rise, through marriage, to a member of a minor aristocratic family.

I think this story makes a fitting contribution to the writing of five members of our maternal Pritchard family, in addition to the tales of my paternal great-grandfather at the beginning of the book.

# CROSSING THE CLASS DIVIDE?
# THE ENIGMA OF MARGARET WILSON BROWN

## by
## Mike Race

'The past is another country' as every family historian knows, and we all explore it in different ways. Knowing that I could trace an ancestor back to 1066 would be wonderful and in the competitive world of genealogy certainly worth a gold medal, but without knowledge of that person, without his or her breath in my face, that knowledge is unfruitful. I decided that in my exploration recent history must come first, the lives of my parents, grandparents, aunts and uncles should be recorded through either the first or second generation (or if you're lucky even the third generation) preferably face to face and in as much detail as possible. The best possible way to record this detail is on audio or video tape or on recently developed digital equipment. We now have the technology to record for ourselves - and for our children and children's children - family voices, and see animated faces, hear tell of family tragedies, triumphs, memories of every aspect of life - health, wealth, childhood, war, old age etc. that will still be seen and listened to in a hundred years' time - we shouldn't let that opportunity slip away. I bitterly regret not taking the opportunity to speak in detail, on tape, to my parents and older relations, twenty five years ago, and am instead recording memories of their lives through the second generation: cousins, nephews and nieces. Remember, tomorrow maybe too late.

I particularly wanted to know about my aunts, my father's three sisters, two of whom, as children, toured the Edwardian music halls, and one of whom, Margaret, appeared to have lived a life that transcended the social barriers of the day. Yet despite living the bulk of their lives in the twentieth century, they are already becoming forgotten figures even within our wider family.

I decided that such an intriguing life as Margaret's shouldn't go unrecorded. So by obtaining, on tape the last fragments of family memories, and carrying out research at the City Archives, Central library, and other more far flung places - and more recently on the internet with help of family – I discovered and have recorded here some of the life of Margaret Wilson Brown (née Race). I start the story at Bishopthorpe in 1948 and then go back to Victorian York, to the home of her grandfather and grandmother, and then her parents, to show the background Margaret came from.

## BISHOPTHORPE, c.1948

As a small boy I was always in awe of Aunt Margaret as, indeed, were some of the more senior members of the family. We, my parents and I, lived in a 'two up and two down' off Lawrence Street which had no bathroom and no hot running water. Aunt Margaret, my father's sister, lived in a mansion (or so it seemed at the time) in Bishopthorpe. She had a large light and airy quarry tiled kitchen, a dining room with a rosewood dining suite, silver cutlery which carried a family crest, oil paintings and French windows. *French windows!* How Agatha Christie, how middle class! There was a lounge with aubergine velvet curtains and a matching three piece suite that snuggled up small boys on winter evenings and left them warm and contented. There was a bathroom with a radiator and endless hot water, and there were large, soft bath towels in which you could envelop yourself. In the hall was a telephone and a musical mug that played 'Do you ken John Peel' when it was (frequently) lifted. There was a large garden with an orchard and long grass where Red Indians - suitably daubed with blackberry war paint - could hide and play for hours. There was a close-cut lawn that was Headingley or Lords to us in the late 1940s summers, where Len Hutton frequently drove Keith Miller's best efforts into the rose beds for four scintillating runs. There was a summer house that smelled, as all summer houses should, of musty deck chairs and old straw hats; last year's newspapers; oiled secateurs and lawnmowers, and drying and decaying plant matter in terracotta plant pots. Aunt Margaret had a gardener. He wore a hat and a waistcoat and was old and bent and might have come straight from a Miss Marple's mystery. She also had a lady who 'did'. My aunt shopped at Harrogate and took the waters there. She looked and sounded like Celia Johnson. Aunt Margaret wore tweeds and twin sets and pearls and had impeccable taste and disciplined speech and an elegant manner.

Our close family gathered at 'Applegarth', Aunt Margaret's house, for most holiday and family celebrations - Christmas, Grandma's birthday etc, (Grandma – Mary Anne Race – was now living with Margaret). Aunt Margaret who came from a family of publicans, corner shop keepers and second hand dealers, had married John Wilson Brown, a relation of Sir Christopher, later Baron Furness, a wealthy ship owner. She had crossed the class divide *–or had she?*

## GEORGE STREET, YORK. 1880

The Albert Inn, George Street, York, June 1880, the beer shop home of Edward Race and his son Arthur Edward, the future father of Margaret Race. Here, I have set down a conversation, based on facts, that might have taken place between Edward and his next door neighbour John Bearpark:

'I'm sorry to see you leave Edward'. John Bearpark and Edward Race had been friends and neighbours for many years. John's wife ran the newsagents and periodical shop next door to 'The Albert'. 'Thanks John, I'm sorry to say goodbye, you've been a good friend'. Indeed John had. Both John and Edward had wives of similar dispositions, strong women who were ambitious to better their circumstances. In John's case running the newsagents had brought extra income, always needed, although he had a good job as a blacksmith at Walker's Iron Foundry in Walmgate. In Edward's case it had brought misery. Shy with strangers he had never enjoyed the life of beer house keeper and had left the business in his wife's hands whilst he continued working as a wheelwright. Edward shuffled his worn boots, 'They haven't exactly been happy days though John, here a' 'T'Albert'. He looked up at the unprepossessing building situated on the corner of Albert and George Street, the beer house name painted in large white letters across the front of the building. 'This place has cost me a wife and a child. It ain't brought happiness'. Oh those painful years! Edward's wife Jane had been dying of phthisis in November 1877 aged 47, knowing that their 14 year old daughter Margaret was pregnant with Henry Etty's child. The arrangements for marriage to Etty at St Margaret's Church on 27$^{th}$ January 1878 when Edward had lied and claimed that Margaret was 17 had been rushed through. Despite the death of their baby boy, Robert, on 7$^{th}$ January 1878 the marriage still went ahead. In September 1878 Margaret entered the County Hospital dying with the disease that had killed her mother. She was unable to bear the regime and discharged herself. She died at home two days later.

John Bearpark nodded his head in sympathy. 'Margaret's ambition never brought you happiness – or wealth - did it?' Edward shook his head. (Unable to match his wife's often unreal expectations, she had come to look down on him. He respected her last wish for a gravestone, but, significantly, nowhere in the inscription did he include the word 'love'). Edward heard boyish shouts from the Peel Street area, and looked round for Arthur, his 10 year old son, but couldn't see him. 'Time we were going John, don't let your missus push you into taking a Walmgate pub, there's not many good houses there.' 'I'll do my best, but you know what she's like!' Edward picked up the handles of his cart, felt the weight, and eased it down again - not too many possessions to be taking to his new lodgings in North Street. He put out his hand, 'All the best John.' He nodded towards the beer house, 'Hope you get on with your new neighbour. His name's Isaac Underwood.' He lifted the cart, set it in motion, and turned for the last time, 'No doubt that lad of mine is playing cricket 'gainst brewery wall a' t'bottom o'George Street, I'll catch up with him there when I cut through t'snicket'. John Bearpark watched as Edward, bowed down, held on tight to the cart as it rattled its way across the cobbles and down George Street. When they reached the Newcastle Arms, he heard Edward shout out, 'Come on Arthur, we have to be getting on…..'

N.B. Isaac Underwood took 'The Albert' when Edward Race departed and immediately changed the name to 'The Shamrock' – an astute move in a mainly Irish Catholic area.

John Bearpark did bow to his wife's ambition, and took a Walmgate pub, The Britannia Inn, in 1883 (more on the Britannia in the next Chapter). His job required much time away from home, and during his absence his daughters began consorting with the customers and eventually became prostitutes. His wife died in 1885, and he was left distraught. Edward Race died in his sleep at lodgings in North Street in January 1883. Although there was room to be buried with his wife, he was buried in a pauper's grave well away from her. In a final humiliation Jane's gravestone was turned, so the austere inscription, 'In memory of Jane Race' (no mention of love or affection) was hidden, and four other non-family members were buried above her, their names added to the back of the stone. In 1891 Edward's son Arthur was living as a lodger with Elizabeth Pritchard and her family in Castlegate York.

## WALMGATE, YORK. 1881

The Britannia Inn, Walmgate, February 1881, the home of Elizabeth and Joe Pritchard and six of their children who still lived with them, included seven year old Mary Ann Pritchard, who was to become the mother of Margaret Race. Here, through some imagination, but mainly research, I have put down a letter Elizabeth Pritchard might have written at the time to her sister Emma in Newcastle:

Dear Emma

It's eleven o'clock in the morning as I write, but the frost is still starring the windows and stiffening the curtains. The Britannia is a cold and draughty place, although with the numbers living here now, we should generate sufficient heat to keep the place warm! We have two new lodgers: one, Jacob Jacops is Polish, a traveller dealing in watches and jewellery, his English is not perfect but despite this, he tells the children wonderful stories of life in Poland. The other, Michel Rhoun, is Irish; warm hearted, but fiery in drink. Outside the draymen are leaving, I can hear the snorting of the horses and the sound of their hooves crunching against the hardened mud. The men are singing, heartened by the odd pint of porter they've had whilst delivering. It has been a difficult winter, the gangs of gaunt, ricketed, Irish urchins from the hovels in Britannia Yard marauding in shoals for sustenance and mischief are even more insolent and desperate this year, and the fire in the tap room can hardly be seen for shivering ill-kempt drinkers. (Drinkers? Three penn'orth of beer seems to last some of them all night). They crowd round it, spitting their phthisis-ridden phlegm into its flames. People say this is a godless place we inhabit, and yes, last week's episode when 40 or more militia men and a great number of wild Irish girls took over the place and couldn't be moved, and stayed 'til dawn - carousing and acting in a most debauched manner - was shameful even for these times. Father Ryan had heard and came and lectured Joe, who protested his innocence, but may well admit it in confession. But these are times when a man and wife must put their children first. With the lodgers we have, and working from dawn to midnight and beyond, we are able to keep the children well fed, clothed and healthy. They are a great blessing to us; all of them strong in mind and body. Christina, now fifteen, strong-willed and fiery, will stand up to any man or woman who insults her and the rest of the them are the same. Mary Ann, the youngest is now seven. Her hair is as red as burnished gold. Like the other girls she is also a strong-willed, determined child and copes well with the life we lead here.....

N.B. In a journal kept by a local magistrate, Joe Pritchard was 'named and shamed' for allowing immoral behaviour in the Britannia Inn. However, the Inn was at the head of Britannia Yard, a notorious Walmgate slum, filled with wild, poverty-stricken Irish immigrants, and keeping a well run house would have been very difficult in these circumstances! Maybe life at the Britannia became too difficult for the Pritchard family, who left to take the Ship Inn in Skeldergate, where Joe died in 1886.

Joe's wife, Elizabeth Pritchard, had a father who had served in the Army for 30 years or more, finally obtaining a position as Librarian at York Barracks. He had two brothers, both soldiers. This may be why she was legendary for her tough character - use of barrack language and a no nonsense approach to life.

## MICKLEGATE, YORK. 1892

Margaret Race was born in 1892 at 33 Micklegate, the eldest daughter of Arthur and Mary Ann Race née Pritchard. Arthur Race was a dairy worker, a 'milk bottler' as stated on his daughter's birth certificate. His wife Mary Ann, a tough determined battler like her mother and many sisters was, like many Victorian mothers, preoccupied in the early days of her marriage in coping with her ever growing family and was unable to provide much added financial support in the early days of her marriage. In consequence of this and Arthur's poor wages the family often had to resort to the soup kitchen. The family frequently moved house. The York electoral registers show the family living at five different addresses around the turn of the 20th Century. Gradually things improved with financial help from other members of the Pritchard family. Mary Ann Race obtained a corner shop in Leeman Road. Margaret and her sister 'Toots' showed ability in entertaining and after auditioning at the 'Empire' joined Cochrane's Children's Troupe and toured the northern music halls for a period of time. However the good times didn't last and in 1905 the family was living in poverty in Castlegate.

## FRIDAY, 21ST MARCH 1905

'How are you Polly?' Leonora May Connor came in through the connecting door that led from No. 3 to No 4 Castlegate. It was 8 o'clock in the morning, and Polly – Mary Ann Race - was already clearing the grate, ready for black leading. Polly pulled her curly red hair back from her face. 'Not too bad May, thanks love.' Leonora May Connor and Polly Race were best pals and had been since that fateful day when Leonora May had arrived from London with her mother and sought lodgings with Elizabeth Pritchard, Polly's mother. Leonora May had much to thank Polly for. She had taken her in to her own home at the newsagents in Bright Street when in 1901 Leonora, newly married and heavily pregnant at 16, was desperate for help, and Polly had witnessed the birth of daughter, also called May.

Leonora May heard the sound of running water, looked into the kitchen and saw Margaret washing her face, her complexion fresh, pink and smooth. 'All right Margaret?' 'Yes thanks May.' Margaret, aged eleven already had a maturity beyond her years. The eldest of the Race children, she had recently returned with her sister from touring the Northern Music Halls with Cochrane's Juveniles Troupe. The money had been a big help to the family, as Polly's husband, Arthur Race, earned a pittance of a wage as a dairyman, and his tendency was to spend his wages in a pub on the way home. One memorable Saturday afternoon returning home drunk, Arthur's wages spent, they only had fish heads for the family Sunday dinner. Polly felt uneasy about the life they lived. It was a wearisome existence, but for all his faults, she loved her husband and family. Although her seven sisters had all married well and prospered, often Polly washed and ironed for some of them to earn extra money – she never regretted her choice in life.

The following pictures the family on one happier day in that year:

'Are you looking forward to coming to the *Empire* tonight Polly?' asked Leonora May. 'I certainly am, wild horses wouldn't keep me away.' The Race's had already had a triumph at an Empire Music Hall talent night, with Margaret and sister 'Toots' winning a cakewalk competition, and tonight the Race children, Margaret, Toots and Arthur were to perform as a concert party group with their uncle Harold Hemmings on violin, Leonora May Connor on piano and her daughter, also May, singing a duet with Arthur; 'I wouldn't leave my little wooden hut for you.' It was Leonora May Connor with her family background in music hall who had started the concert party and had also been instrumental in getting the Race girls into the Cochrane Juveniles.

N.B. I interviewed 99 year old May Passmore née Connor in 2000 for a York Oral History Society project. To my astonishment I found that her grandmother had lodged with Elizabeth Pritchard, my great-grandmother in Stonegate in the 1890s, and May herself was born in Bright Street, the newsagent's home of my Grandparents Arthur and Mary Ann Race. Her parents – with May – lived with the Races' for some years, forming a deep friendship that lasted throughout their lives. I gained intimate and informative information from May concerning the trials, tribulations and triumphs of the Race family in the early years of the 20$^{th}$ Century. May Passmore came from a fascinating family of music hall entertainers, and led a life rich in incident and interest.

## 1911 TO 1942. THE MYSTERY YEARS

I know that Margaret attended English Martyrs Roman Catholic school with the rest of her brothers and sisters and that she worked for an aunt, Agnes Stanislaus Stabler and her husband Charles, who ran the 'Coach and Horses' public house in Nessgate when she first left school, and is named in the 1911 census as a barmaid there. After that little is known of her life until 1942 when she married. Many of the family believe that she worked in nursing perhaps doing private work. Eileen Wood, an older cousin who was close to Margaret when she returned to York in the 1940s, said that when she was a young girl she was taken by Aunt Margaret to Harrogate and Leeds on shopping expeditions, to buy clothes. She was told that Basil Sydney, a well known actor, was my aunt's friend. Eileen also said that Aunt Margaret told her she was 'never to neglect the refinements of life.' She insisted on good manners, and taught her how to address people on meeting them. Eileen, and another cousin, also recalled Margaret saying that she had trained or worked at Guy's Hospital (although I have a 1920's photograph of her with friends, reputed to be taken at Guys, I haven't yet obtained hard evidence of this). They also said that Margaret may have worked as an hotel book-keeper and that she had a flat in Yeadon near Leeds. I know she lived in the Leeds area for some years. I have seen a signature in a book by Dorothy Una Radcliffe the Yorkshire writer and socialite based in Leeds, that carries an inscription 'For Margaret Race – so long'. This might have been her, and suggests some kind of working relationship.

The next certainty is that she married John Wilson Brown, a timber merchant with interests in Scandinavia. I know that she married him in York Register Office on 2nd November 1942. I also know that he died in 1943 and that in 1943-44 she was living as his widow in the Brown family home 'Woodlands' in West Hartlepool.

N.B. Like many of her aunts and their husbands who ran well-kept city centre pubs, Agnes Stanislaus and Charles Stabler, who ran one of the largest licensed premises in York, will have made a good living. (A number of Margaret's cousins were privately educated, including attending finishing schools in France). Agnes and Charles were childless and may well have funded Margaret's Further Education, whether in bookkeeping or nursing).

The Brown's: Margaret's husband John Wilson Brown came from a distinguished family. His grandfather John was the Mayor of Hartlepool, his father Christopher, a J.P., married Eliza Furness the sister of Sir Christopher, later Baron Furness, a powerful and wealthy ship owner and Liberal M.P. (1891-1900). The Browns lived in a 30 roomed house with large grounds which was visited by Princess Mary in 1926 during her visit to Hartlepool. They had a chauffeur and a retinue of servants. There has also been speculation that the house was used for assignations by Edward (David) Prince of Wales and his future wife Wallis Simpson.

## CONCLUSIONS

When a boy, my father told me that Aunt Margaret was the widow of a rich timber merchant from West Hartlepool, who on his death had left his fortune to build a ward in the town's hospital, but had granted Margaret sufficient money to live a comfortable life as a widow. They had no children. That was it. This was the time when discretion still ruled within society, secrets were kept, family matters were hidden from outsiders. There was still shame in behaviour that didn't conform to the rules of the day, family ties were strong, and closed ranks were the order for dealing with family scandals. I didn't start to investigate Margaret's life until all her immediate family – her mother, brothers and sisters

– were dead. As I've written earlier, I have since spoken to an older female cousin who was close to her, who told me of her good taste, how she educated her in etiquette and manners. Others also told me that they thought she married in the 1920s and shared the gilded life of the middle classes of that time. Alas, they, and I, were to be sadly disillusioned.

After fruitless searches of the national marriage records for the 1920s and '30s, I eventually came across the marriage of Margaret Race and John Wilson Brown in 1942, one year before his death in 1943. Her marriage had been witnessed by her mother and her sister, who had never revealed the secret to any other members of the family. Conjecture must have it that John and Margaret had shared their lives for years before their marriage, but that the gulf in their social backgrounds was too great to bridge until he was dying. My aunt was an intelligent, articulate, attractive woman, but still not good enough to marry a man born into privilege. I find much offensive about today's society but perhaps if Margaret and John had been living today the recognition that love can now transcend the class divide might have brought them contentment and perhaps – who knows - a family of their own?

Margaret died on 17th March 1968 taking her memories and secrets to the grave undisclosed. As an oral and family history researcher, I have enjoyed searching out as much as I can about her. I think she would be surprised if she knew how much I'd found out from public documents, computer data, various publications, and people – some of whom she knew – and others she never met. My appetite for the truth about my enigmatic aunt is still not sated, so my research will continue until all the doors are closed.

Margaret Race on right, with friends

The Brown family c.1905
John Wilson Brown seated far right, with his parents,
brother and sisters

# TRUTH IS STRANGER THAN FICTION

## BY

## JANET PIGOTT

Janet Pigott (née Taylor) with proofs of her first book

# INTRODUCTION

Having read stories written or recalled by my family members, readers will probably expect to find some tales of my own. These are offered as memoirs, in the pages which follow. All of them are genuine. Some are presented as dualogues, others as short stories. Some are as a result of being given topic headings at the writing group which I joined.. The story about the missing R is one of these. It started as my attempt to write a short story from a page of newspaper advertisements for 'Houses For Sale' where we were asked to select one of the properties and write a short story about it. What sort of people lived in it? Why were they selling it? What was it like inside the house? What type of people would want to buy it? In reality it developed into an intriguing mystery which I was determined to solve.

Some of my memoirs reflect my involvement with my dear Mum when I visited her or took her for appointments as she got older. They are told with no disrespect to her, just love and incredulity. I hope readers will enjoy them as much as I did when writing them down immediately after they happened.

Other stories recall things drawn from my memory of long ago. Like my forebears, I seem to have a long-standing memory which can recall things from yester-year, when triggered. I have enjoyed putting them together for this final section of the book.

# 1 ~ A TERRIFIED TRIO
## by
## Janet Pigott

Bombs rained down onto rows of terraced houses, whistling, zooming, exploding, detonating when they made contact with properties and the streets below. They split open roofs, smashed houses to smithereens, and created craters in the dank gassy earth, which smelt of sulphur and burning rags. The noise was stupendous: thundering, roaring, rumbling, whizzing, cracking, terrifying. Some missiles missed, others scored targets. We were petrified by the unforgiving attack.

Three of us huddled in the cupboard under their stairs, our torches flickering in the dimly lit hole. We looked unsightly in our black and grey gas masks with our hands clasped over our ears, hearts pounding, terrified for our lives, as debris crashed down all around us. The atmosphere was heavy with brick-dust. We could hardly breathe through the heavily laden smoke and fumes.

With one almighty blast my Grandmother and Mum lost their hearing. Their ears were numbed and silenced forever.

Shock waves tremored through the air as house-bricks, rubble and huge chunks of wood fell to the ground, splintering, and barring our escape route. The cupboard door was wedged tightly shut. We were trapped.

Forty-five minutes later, only I could hear the 'all-clear' sirens.

Mum, Grandma and I trembled and gripped each other's hands tightly. We cried and screamed for help in the hope that Wardens would hear and rescue us from our plight. How would we escape, if at all? The planes had gone for that particular air raid, but they would be back another day. Would we survive another attack? Where would we live if we did escape? How would we cope?

These memories of an air attack in WWII still haunt me from time to time; but we did survive, and all three of us lived to tell the tale.

# 2 ~ MY FIRST MEMORY

A pair of fawn-coloured zip-up slippers shuffling inch by inch across a maroon and grey floral carpet square carried my eyes up to the wearer, my Great-Grandfather, Frederick Oscar Finlayson, aged 95. His sturdy mahogany walking stick never left him. He trailed it across the mat, leaning heavily on it as he made his way out of the room.

I was sitting on the floor playing with an empty cotton-reel, pushing it, to see if I could make it reach the dark brown linoleum surrounds. When it did, I whooped with joy. I doubt whether a child of 4 would get as much pleasure from such a simple activity nowadays!

As Great-Grandpa passed me, I looked up at him. The most noticeable features of his face were his well-trimmed moustache and bushes of white whiskers around each of his jowls.

In a gentlemanly gesture, he touched the peak of his smart tweed cap, which he wore at all times and never removed from my sight; not even at the meal table! He was well dressed in a dark blue and red checked winceyette shirt, with a navy-blue tie and cardigan, and thick navy blue serge trousers. He was a very old, well cared for, gentleman.

One day when we were seated at the tea-table I felt a sudden sharp pain on the back of my hand. I howled and drew my left hand from where it was resting on the immaculately laundered white Damask tablecloth. My Geordie grandmother instantly jumped up from her seat and chastised him:

"Eeee, Pa, divant dee that ti the bairn, it's not nice!"

"Had-a-wayer, Hinny, ah divant dee anything, ti the wean," he retorted.

My hand smarted. I cried. He had stirred his cup of hot tea with a spoon, then rested it on the back of my left hand.

"It's rude to put your hands on the table at mealtimes. Please divant dee it any more, hinny"

In the year in which he lived after that incident, as far as I can remember he never did it again and I always remembered my manners in his presence. He hadn't meant to hurt me on that occasion, he just intended to teach me to take my hands off the tablecloth.

Occasionally when we visited him in my Grandmother's house, in Newcastle-on Tyne, I would sit beside him whilst he told me stories about when he went to sea as a young man, serving on Missionary Ships in the South Sea Islands. He spoke with a mellow Geordie dialect which I loved to try and imitate.

Everyone was proud of Frederick Oscar Finlayson, "FOF" or "Pa", as they called him, and I loved and respected him.

He was a wonderful old man and to this day I cherish his memory with affection and fondness.

# 3 ~ CHILDHOOD MEMORIES

It was 1943. I wore a dark brown beret, a fawn coat and a home-made label around my neck, which bore the words: "TO BE COLLECTED AT NEWCASTLE CENTRAL STATION". On the back of the label was the name and address of my paternal grandmother.

Mum held my right hand, and carried a leather suitcase with her other hand. We walked to the station together – a place I already knew because I had done this journey before.

We entered the concourse, which was heaving with groups of soldiers. Long tubular kit-bags littered the ground. Some women wore their hair caught up in snoods, some had pageboy hair styles. Some wore headscarves so I couldn't see their hair at all. They kissed or clung to uniformed men. A lot of the women were crying.

Mum threaded her way through them all, and bought a child's return and a platform ticket. We went through the ticket barrier where a man clipped both tickets, and queried the latter. She explained that I would be travelling on my own; and she would ask the guard to find me a suitable seat on the train. We crossed a footbridge and stood on platform 9. There, a few elderly women wearing sombre felt hats and tweed coats stood with elderly men, or comforted young soldiers, until the large, black, dusty steam engine chugged slowly up the track, until the last coach reached us.

Mum made me stand well back so that I wouldn't be sucked in by the draft the train caused as the engine's noisy brakes screeched to a standstill. We walked to the guard's van and she talked to the guard. Together they took me to a corner seat in a compartment next to his van. There were two upholstered bench seats opposite each other. They sat me in the corner seat next to the window, with my back to the engine so that specks of soot wouldn't get in my eyes in the event of a passenger opening a small window at the top of the much larger one.

People surged into the compartment and an elderly couple sat opposite me. Two soldiers sat on the bench next to them, and three men in a different kind of uniform – ones I'd never seen before – came and sat next to me. Their uniforms were a greyish-blue with little embroidered wings at the top of their sleeves. They wore hats that looked far too small for their heads and were cocked at a rakish angle. They carried magazines and a newspaper which I heard one of them refer to as "Titbits". All the men lifted their luggage onto a shelf above their heads, but some of the kitbags were too bulky, so they stood them on the floor. Mum put her suitcase underneath the window.

The guard said: 'This little girl is going to Newcastle Central Station, and I shall be keeping an eye out for her grandmother when she gets there; so please would you make sure she doesn't get off at Darlington or Durham.'

Approving his assertive tone, Mum turned to me:

'Now you be a good girl. Behave yourself. Look after Grandma and remember to flush the toilet when you've used it. I have to go now. Ta-ta.' She kissed me on my forehead and disappeared into the corridor which was packed with servicemen standing up. A few seconds later I saw her on the platform with several other women, all waving goodbye to their loved ones as the engine let off steam, whistled, and slowly puffed out of the station. I had no fear about travelling on my own. I'd done it once before when the war was on and Grandma had been there to meet me then, so I knew she would be there again this time.

During the journey the two soldiers fell asleep. The old man read a book, and the other three men thumbed through their magazines and papers. I looked out of the window. Telegraph poles passed by with steamy, smoky, regularity. Their wires danced up and down the windowpane. Fields and hedges floated by. Cows laid in groups; sheep nibbled the grass. There was no sign of a war there.

The old lady asked how old I was. I told her I was four-and-a-half. She asked about my Mum, and why I was travelling alone. I told her I was going for a little holiday with my Grandma whilst Mum went into hospital. When Grandma brought me back, Mum would give me a nice present if I'd been good.

The old lady looked concerned. She asked if I said my prayers.

'Oh, yes,' I replied. 'Every night I pray that God will keep Mum and Daddy safe, and bring Daddy safely home to us.'

Then she asked if I ever looked at the moon before I went to sleep.

'Sometimes I do, when it's dark at night, but it's not always there, especially on light nights.'

'Oh yes it is, dear. It's just that you can't always see it because it's covered with clouds, or it's too light in the summer, but it's always there. So the next time you look at the moon and see it shining brightly, remember that it's not only shining on you, it's also shining on your Mum – and your Daddy – wherever he is. That knowledge will bring all three of you much closer together.'

We chattered for the remainder of the journey, and when we arrived at Newcastle Grandma was on the platform to meet me.

We travelled to her house in a dark-brown coloured tramcar through the town area, and transferred to a grey trolley bus to the suburbs. When we arrived at her house, my 95-year old Great-grandpa was there and welcomed me with open arms. He was a grand old man and I loved him dearly. Grandpa wasn't there because he was serving in the Merchant Navy. Later that evening my unmarried Auntie came home from work. She was lovely. She played the piano a lot. That night she played my favourite pieces to me – The Teddy Bear's Picnic, and In a Monastery Garden. I loved to hear the part where the bells chimed, and asked her to play the pieces over and over again. Then it was time for bed.

I stayed in Newcastle for two weeks, before Grandma took me home. I'd been promised that if I was a good girl Mum would give me a nice present when we got back. She may have thought it was a nice present, but I didn't! What she gave me was a baby brother that was too tiny to play with, and woke me up at night when he cried to be fed. But when I said my prayers, I added his name to theirs; and when I looked at the moon shining in the sky at night, I knew my Mum and my Daddy would be pleased with me because I'd been a very good girl while I was away.

I also prayed for the war to end and for Daddy to come home safely, but it took another three years before those prayers were answered.

# 4 ~ HOLIDAY IN FILEY

I was almost 8 years old when I met my Dad for the second time. He was called for WWII service when I was 14 months old, and was demobbed in December 1946.

I don't remember Dad coming home. He must have arrived in the night whilst I was asleep. Mum told me, years later, that I was jealous of him and said "Send that man away," but I don't remember saying it, and I don't remember being prepared for his home coming. What I do remember, though, is an incident which happened when I was four years old.

When Dad came home on leave Mum and Dad took me to Filey for a week's holiday. Dad was attentive and kind to me. He took me paddling in the sea and paid for me to have a donkey ride across the beach. We made sand-castles, and played with a bucket and spade whilst Mum sat on a waterproof sheet and watched us.

I also remember his concern on the second morning of our stay when I locked myself in the lavatory of the guest-house where we were staying. I had shot the bolt, and couldn't get it out again. Both parents stood on the landing and gave me instructions to put my finger in the little circular latch-hole and pull hard, but I didn't have the strength to release the bolt. Time passed. I cried. I screamed. I panicked. I thought I was locked in for ever. Try as I might, the bolt wouldn't shift!

After what seemed to be a very long time I was aware of noises at the back of the lavatory pan. A ladder had been located and was placed underneath the tiny window. My parents told me to stand as close to the door as possible. A window-cleaner had been found and he would come and rescue me. Presently I saw a finger and thumb appear through the small gap between the upper and lower windows. It grappled to find the release hole in the bar which held it in place on the catch. With an almighty tug the top window was released and pushed up. But the window-cleaner was too big to get through the gap. He went back down the ladder.

I sat on the floor in the corner of the little room and sobbed my heart out. Dad spoke kindly to me from the other side of the door. He told me not to be frightened. The window cleaner had gone to get some tools and was going to have to break the glass in the lower window so that he could get through to undo the lock. I was terrified. What if I bled to death from flying glass? I cowered and covered my head with my hands when the man came back up the ladder again.

Hammering, shattering, sawing went on. The lower window frame was removed. The man squeezed and crawled through the gap he'd created. His hands were bleeding. His boiler-suit was ripped around the knees. He unlocked the door saying: "Who's a naughty girl, then?"

I fled into the open arms of my Daddy who was still waiting on the landing outside the toilet. He hugged me and told me that everything would be all right, but never to lock myself in again.

Despite his consoling words and loving arms around me, everything was not all right. The window had to be replaced the same day and the broken glass and mess cleared away. Mum and Dad were presented with the bill for the work to be carried out. It meant that after paying cash for the repairs they didn't have enough money left to pay for the remainder of the holiday. That night they packed their cases and next morning we went home, much to both parents' disappointment.

We arrived home about 3 pm, just as a motor-cyclist was approaching the house where we lived. He dismounted and gave Dad a telegram. His leave had been cancelled and he had to return to duty immediately. He couldn't believe the words on the paper. It was as if fate had intended him to be there at that particular time.

The next day we all went back to the station. Mum cried. I cried. Dad was bottled up with emotion. We watched the train depart; stood on the platform and waved until it was out of sight. Our holiday was well and truly over. In later years, I often wondered what would have happened if Dad hadn't been there to receive that demanding telegram.

When Dad finally returned from the War he was a different man. He was older, slower, and bald. Not only had he lost his hair, he had lost his sense of humour. He was meticulous in his attention to detail, and serious in his attitude to life. But he never stopped loving Mum and me, and found additional love for us all – including his son – who was, by that time, a healthy three year old.

# 5 ~ A DAY OUT ON MY OWN

When WWII was over there were occasions when the smell of Rowntree's chocolate wafted over the rooftops of the little terrace houses, where I lived with my mother, in a small cul-de-sac of eight houses – four on each side of Belgrave Street – near Haxby Road Infants' School in York.

On the day of the trip to my maternal grandmother's house, it was one of those delicious-smelling days. The sun was shining, it was a beautifully warm day, and my tummy was full from the third of a pint of milk which we'd been made to drink at morning playtime.

The milk came in metal crates, which contained about 30 small glass bottles each topped with a white cardboard waxed disk which could be depressed slightly in the middle to create a small circular hole into which a drinking-straw was placed by a "milk monitor". The milk laid heavily on my stomach and I didn't want to run or play for several hours after drinking it. So that was the situation I was in on the day I walked three miles, on my own, to find my Mum.

A neighbour's son, Alec Wales, and I walked home from school together at lunch-time. He went into his house where the door was closed, but unlocked, and I walked a few steps further on to ours. The door was also closed, but very firmly locked and there was no reply. I hammered on the door and shouted for Mummy to open it, but there was no response from within.

My yelling and banging attracted the attention of a woman who lived across the road, and she came out into the street to see what was going on. She was of enormously-built proportions. Her two unsupported "top tummies" rolled about under her dress which was covered with a dirty Paisley-patterned wraparound apron. Her blonde hair was matted and she held a lighted cigarette in one hand whilst leaning her other hand on the door frame. Mum had warned me never to repeat the words she used because she said many of them were swear words which mustn't be used by little children. The woman's tone was always loud and abrasive. I found her stance in the doorway frightening. She told me that my 'effing' mother had gone to the chip shop in the next street. So I decided to go to meet her, rather than wait by the front door of our back-to-back house with this gross loud-mouthed woman watching and swearing at me.

When I got to the shop, Mummy wasn't there, and I hadn't passed her en-route. At first I didn't know what to do! I stood there for a while and eventually decided that she must have gone to see her mother, my maternal Grandma, who lived at the other side of the City.

The year after my brother had been born Mummy, pushing him in a big black Marmet-Clyder pram, (which she'd bought second-hand) and with me clinging to the handle, had walked across the City, and back, every other Sunday afternoon when we visited my Grandma for tea – so I knew the route by heart.

Instead of going back home and waiting for her, I walked down Wiggington Road, into Clarence Street, down Gillygate; crossed the busy main Bootham Road and into Exhibition Square. At the Art Gallery I developed an itch in my bottom, so I lifted my skirt and scratched it. Some people waiting at a bus-stop smiled and tittered, but no-one said anything to me.

I continued into Duncombe Place where I thought they hadn't finished building the big church called The Minster, because there was still scaffolding up!

I skipped down Blake Street, through St. Helen's Square, down Coney Street, and into Spurriergate. There was a policeman on traffic duty as I crossed the road at Nessgate, but he took no notice of me; he was far too busy.

Then I walked along Tower Street, where I stopped for a few minutes to gaze at the imposing Clifford's Tower where Mum had previously told me that Roman soldiers used to throw people to the lions in days gone by. I thought that was very cruel. I shuddered. A creepy feeling went up my spine as I visualised terrified people screaming as they were thrown and being eaten alive. I imagined the sound of their bones being crunched, and ran on until I came to the river Ouse as it speeded its way under Skeldergate Bridge. Through the small ornate gaps in the parapet of the iron bridge, I watched whirlpools forming and dissipating in the murky flow of water below.

After resting at the bridge I was ready to tackle the final leg of my journey up Bishopgate Street into Bishopthorpe Road. I dawdled past a line of shops where I stopped and peered into their windows; then turned right into Scarcroft Road, and finally arrived at Grandma's house in Scott Street. Her front door was unlocked; I pushed it open and went inside her house.

Grandma was amazed to see me; but Mummy wasn't with her. Grandma hadn't seen her since the previous Sunday.

After sitting me down for a little while to have a rest, she gave me another a drink of milk, and 2 biscuits. Grandma was very deaf and didn't always correctly lip-read the answers I gave to her questions.

Eventually she gave me a sixpenny piece and told me to go to the bus stop on Bishopthorpe Road and get a bus to the station. Then I had to ask the conductress to show me where the bus stop was for a bus to Haxby Road, and go straight home to Mummy whom, she said, would be worried about me.

When I got home, Mum was very angry. Her eyes were swollen with tears. Her face contorted as she shrieked at me. She wanted to know where I'd been, and what I'd been doing. She wailed that she'd been frantic with worry, and had informed the Police. She threatened that if I ever went off on my own again she would smack me very hard indeed. I was petrified. I didn't know what I'd done wrong. I'd only gone to look for her, and when she wasn't at the chip shop or Grandma's I'd come straight back on the bus as instructed. I thought she'd be glad to see me!

When I'd stopped crying, and said I was sorry, she made some scrambled egg from yellow powder out of a silver-coloured tall tin with blue print on the outside. It was powdered egg and she reconstituted a large spoonful and cooked it in a pan on the top of the old gas oven. I'd only just finish eating it when Grandma turned up. She said she'd been worried about me and rued not bringing me back personally. She wondered whether I'd got home safely, so had followed me on the next sequence of buses.

What surprised them both, and what they didn't understand, is how I'd remembered the route and the fact that not a solitary person had stopped me, an infant-school child, from walking through the town and crossing busy main roads on my own without an adult with me during school hours. And what I didn't understand, and never found out, is where Mummy had been – and why the house didn't smell of chips.

# 6 ~ THE CARDIAC MACHINE

| | |
|---|---|
| Cardiologist | Violet, We're going to record your heart-beat on this little tape-recorder. You must wear it for 24 hours. Don't try to take it off. We'll take it off at 3 o'clock tomorrow. |
| Violet | Well what do I do when I want to go to sleep? |
| Cardiologist | You just go to sleep with it on. |
| Violet | Won't it hurt me if I lie on it? |
| Cardiologist | You can't lie on it because it's at the front of your body, on your tummy. But if you like just put it to the side and it will lie on the bed. You can't hurt it, and it can't hurt you. |
| Violet | Oh! Well what do I do if I want to go the toilet? |
| Cardiologist | You just get up and go. You can walk about with it on. The tape recorder is inside a little bag on this strap, so when you get up to go to the toilet it goes with you. You're not plugged into a wall socket. The machine goes by itself. You don't have to take it off. You just get up and go to the toilet normally. |
| Violet | Oh. I see. Now I understand. |

## VISITING HOUR SAME TIME THE NEXT DAY

| | |
|---|---|
| Janet | Hello, Mum. How are you today? |
| Violet | I'm very worried. This little bag hasn't gone yet. |
| Janet | Well it's only just twenty-four hours since they put it on, they'll be coming to take it off very soon, I expect. |
| Violet | But it hasn't done its job yet! It hasn't worked. |
| Janet | How do you know it hasn't worked? |

| | |
|---|---|
| Violet | Because it hasn't moved my bowels yet. The lady said when I wanted to go, it would go for me. But it hasn't worked. I'm still waiting to go. |
| Janet | No, Mum. She said when you wanted to go to the toilet the bag would go WITH you because it is strapped to your body. It's there to monitor your heart-beat. It's got nothing to do with your bowels. Anyway, I've brought you some stewed rhubarb so perhaps that may help? |
| Violet | I certainly hope so. I like to go every day if I can. What with this little bag and your rhubarb, surely one of them will work soon! |

# 7 ~ THE LIGHT IN THE DARK

It was October 1958. I was an officer of the Girl Guide Company in Bishopthorpe village, where the Archbishop of York's Palace is situated. Every Friday, after the age of 18, I cycled through a twisty, unlit road, approximately two miles to the hall where we held our meetings.

Mrs Rix was our Guide Captain and I was her Lieutenant. In addition to our weekly meetings, we had great fun camping under canvas and loved to have camp-fire sing-songs.

From 1956 to 1961 His Grace Archbishop Ramsey was the incumbent at the Palace. He was a large-framed, charitable man who supported many local events. On one occasion he invited us to hold a camp-fire in the Palace grounds. He instructed his gardener to choose a suitable site on the perimeter of the grounds, and dig out a two-metre square of turf which could be replaced the next day when the cold ashes of the fire were removed.

On the occasion of the camp-fire the Guide Company met at the Church Hall at 7 pm, as usual. We took a roll-call, gathered together a supply of ground-sheets to sit on, and walked the short distance to the Palace entrance. The gardener was there to greet us and guided us to the spot where we were to entertain ourselves.

It was dusk, but we quickly placed our groundsheets down, and the girls sat on them. Then Mrs Rix and I put a pile of kindling in the centre of the prepared square and surrounded it with a wigwam of dried twigs.

Several of the Guides had been to the Hilly Fields on the banks of the River Ouse earlier that week and had collected a supply of fallen branches ready to build the fire into a vibrant centrepiece. A match was lit. Flames rose. The fire caught hold. We built it up to a sizable mound, and sang to our heart's content.

The Archbishop came to see that we were enjoying ourselves. We lustily sang *'Ging-Gang-Goolly'*; and *'Over an Ocean of Sparkling Snow'*;

then sweetly sang '*Kum-by-Yah, my Lord*' for him before he said a prayer, blessed us, and departed.

The light changed from dusk to dark. After singing a few more campfire songs we finished with our 'Taps' which we always sang at the close of our meetings. Mrs Rix walked back to the village with the group of Guides.

One of the older girls, Elizabeth Standing, who lived with her parents in a flat in the converted stable block, stayed with me to douse out the dying embers with cold water so that there could be no lighted ashes to cause damage overnight. As we checked everything was all right, I suddenly saw a light moving in the distance. It was low to the ground. Sometimes it moved slowly. Sometimes it was stationary. Sometimes it moved up and down. Sometimes it disappeared and re-appeared. I was puzzled by the movements and drew Elizabeth's attention to it.

"Can you see that light over there, Elizabeth? What is it?"

"Oh, it's nothing to worry about! It's only Timothy Tanquerey."

"No, I don't think it's a person. It's too low. I mean that light down near the ground."

"Yes, that's right. The Archbishop's wife, Mrs Ramsey, has a companion called Miss Tanquerey. She has a dog called Timothy. Miss Tanquerey doesn't like going out in the dark at night, so when Timothy wants to go out for his call of nature, she switches on a torch and fixes it to his collar so that when she puts him out on his own he can see where he's going."

"You're kidding me?"

"Would I do that, Leffy? No! It's perfectly true."

When we were satisfied that the ashes were cold we parted company and I cycled alone down that dark twisting road, grateful for the light which my bike's dynamo provided as I pedalled my way safely home.

# 8 ~ A MISUNDERSTANDING IN VERONA

One hot afternoon, during a trip to Verona, Peter and I found a corner café, with two people seated at one table and one person at another. About twenty empty tables were available. They were all set with four place settings, but they were situated in searingly hot sunshine. In the shade, however, there was one table set with six place settings, so we sat at it and waited to be served. A waiter came and took our order for two cups of tea with milk one toasted cheese sandwich and one ice-cream. We waited patiently to be served. Eventually a young Italian waiter approached us.

| | |
|---|---|
| Waiter | Sawree. Can't serve you here. This table for six. You are two. You have to move. |
| Peter | We prefer to sit in the shade, it's very hot in the sun. |
| Waiter | No. This is table for more than two. You have to move. |
| | *We moved to the next table set for four people. There was a local seascape picture printed on a piece of paper towel roll on it – which the waiter picked up, scrumpled, and threw into a waste-bin.* |
| Janet | Oh, that's a pity, I would have liked that for a souvenir. |
| | *Ten minutes passed by before the waiter came back, but we were glad to sit down and have a rest after our long walk.* |
| Waiter | Sawree. No ice-cream. Ice-cream off. |
| Peter | Then I'll have an iced drink – strawberry flavour please. |
| | *Five more minutes passed by.* |
| Waiter | Sawree. No strawberry. Banana or Ananas. |

| | |
|---|---|
| Peter | Ananas – that's pineapple. I'll have that please. |
| | *Another 5 minutes passed by, then the waiter returned with part of our order – 2 cups of tea but no milk; the pineapple drink, but no toasted cheese sandwich.* |
| Janet | Could we have some milk for our tea please? |
| Waiter | Sawree. No milk. Milk off. Lemon only. |
| Janet | No lemon thank you. We'll have the tea as it is. But before you go, can I ask you something? When we arrived there was a picture on the table. That lady over there has one, and that couple also have one. Could I have a picture for my souvenir scrapbook please? |
| Waiter | Picture? What is picture? I don't understand. |
| Janet | When we arrived there was a picture on the table. You crumpled it up and put it in that bin. |
| | *I wrung my hands to show a crumpling motion, followed by a throwing gesture towards the waste bin.* |
| Waiter | Oh, now I understand. You want to wash your hands! |
| | *Peter got up and took a piece of printed towel roll with a picture of Verona printed on it from a nearby table.* |
| Husband | This is the picture. Could we have one of these please, to put in our scrap book? |
| Waiter | Oh, Picture! **Picture**! For you, Madam? You have it! |
| Peter | Thank You. |
| Janet | Thank you. Success at last! |
| | *But we never did get the milk or the toasted cheese sandwich.* |

# 9 ~ EAVESDROPPING

| | |
|---|---|
| Peter | Jan's been on that laptop all day. I hardly ever see her. |
| Friend | What does she do on it? Does she research Family History? |
| Peter | No. She writes short stories. |
| Friend | Oh, really! What sort of short stories? What genre? |
| Peter | Anything. She goes to Pens of Erdington twice a month. The mentor is highly motivating, full of pizzazz and spirit and it rubs off on her. She comes home elated and spends the next day or two doing her homework, typing up her notes, and launching into the topic allocated. I hardly ever see her. |
| Friend | That must be very difficult for you? |
| Peter | No, it isn't – because I'm on the computer upstairs! |

# 10 ~ THE MISSING R

At the writing group which I attend, we were given a page of advertisements for house sales advertised in a newspaper, and asked to select one and write a story about it.

I chose to write about a house alleged to have belonged to Richmal Crompton, the author of the Just William Stories, I believed it was as genuine as its description. I could imagine it filled with antique furniture and book-cases full of 'Just William' stories and other books, but once I got home and started looking in reference books to find out more about her, I realised there was no way she ever lived there, or owned it.

For one thing, I discovered that her real name was Richmal Crompton Lamburn, and if the house was built for her in 1906, she would have only been 16 years of age at that time, and still be a pupil at St Elphin's School for daughters of the Clergy in Lancashire. She would neither have had the money, nor the legal ability to buy it. I was intrigued. I felt it would help my assignment if I could find out more about the house and the people who were selling it.

From my local library, I managed to borrow a copy of Richmal's official biography, by Mary Cadogan, published in 1986. It was very interesting. I went through it with a fine tooth comb but despite finding that Richmal had lived in, or bought, 12 different properties I could find no evidence of any connection with the house currently being advertised as being built for her in Bromley, Kent.

I also researched information about her on the Internet. I was interested to read that Richmal started at St. Elphin's school in Warrington, Lancashire, at the age of 11, in 1901, where she joined her older sister, Gwen. But three years later the pupils and teachers moved to Darley Dale after a severe outbreak of Scarlet Fever, and the premises were condemned as being unfit because of the drains.

From there, Richmal went to The Royal Holloway College at Egham in Englefield Green, Surrey until 1914. After she attained her Degree, she went back to St Elphin's for three years and became a successful classics teacher.

In 1915 Richmal's father died under anaesthetic while having a minor operation, and left his entire estate to his wife. By that time Gwen had married and moved to live with her husband, Thomas Disher, in Bromley, Kent. As she didn't like living alone, Mrs Lamburn went to live with them. This unsettled Richmal and she decided that when her three year commitment to the Headmistress in Darley Dale was up, she would try and find a teaching post in Kent, to be nearer to her family. She was successful in finding a job as a classics teacher at Bromley High School and bought a house in Cherry Orchard Road in a district called Bromley Common.

In addition to her day job, Richmal took to writing stories, so Mrs Lamburn left Gwen and Thomas' home and went to live with Richmal in order to help her with her housework. Her first published story was in 1918, in Girls' Own Paper. After that, a series of 12 *Just William* stories for children was published in magazines and they were a huge success.

In 1923 Richmal developed a virulent cold. Her mother took her to Cromer in Norfolk to recuperate, but she got worse. She was diagnosed as having poliomyelitis, and lost the use of her right leg. She must have been devastated. On doctor's orders she had to give up her teaching career, and when she was well enough, turned her hand to full-time writing.

By 1927 Richmal had saved enough money to have a new house built – The Glebe, in Oakley Road, Bromley Common, but once more, tragedy struck her life. In the 1930's she developed breast cancer and had a mastectomy. Her mother continued to live at The Glebe and cared for her, until her own death in 1939. In the early 1950's Richmal moved from The Glebe to a house called 'Beechworth' in Chislehurst, Kent, in which she died on 16th January 1969.

So what was her connection with the property advertised as having been built for her in 1906?

In an attempt to complete my assignment for the writing group, I telephoned the Estate Agents. The house was still on the market. I spoke with a person who asked if I was interested in buying it. I replied that unfortunately I wasn't, but I *was* interested in its history, and asked to be sent a copy of the sales brochure. As I was not a prospective purchaser I was told my request could not be fulfilled. I was astounded at the reply.

I said I was working on an assignment for a writing group and knew that Richmal was only 16 years of age in 1906 so she couldn't have had the house built for both legal and financial reasons, and she didn't go to live in Bromley until 1917. I heard a deep intake of breath. Then it was suggested that the house might have been built as a home for the family rather than for the author, but I felt sure this wasn't true.

Like a dog with a bone, I was determined to find out more about the house and asked if I couldn't have a brochure, could I be given a verbal description over the phone, as I needed to create an atmosphere and characters for my story. The young woman helped by describing the seven-bedroomed house, the servants' bell system in the kitchen, and the piano in the window.

I asked myself why would a disabled person want to live in a seven bedroomed house? Perhaps it was a status symbol for her? Perhaps it was to satisfy her ego that she was somebody of substance? Perhaps it was to maintain a distinguished home where publishers could visit her and draw up contracts for her writing because she couldn't get to them very easily with her paralysed leg? Perhaps it was somewhere she could entertain family members regularly? It was a mystery! Why should the Estate Agents claim that Richmal had it built in 1906 when she was still a schoolgirl? My telephone call had raised more questions than answers!

Several days later I had the inspiration to contact the Land Registry Office in Bromley. Surely they would be able to tell me for whom the house had been built in 1906? I spoke with a nice-sounding man. He told me that although land registry started in some parts of London in 1876 the majority of properties were not registered until the 1950's. He advised me to write a letter of enquiry, bullet-pointing things I wanted to know, and someone would check the files. I wrote and posted my letter that very afternoon.

I was delighted to receive a prompt reply but disappointed that documentation could not be found concerning Richmal Crompton Lamburn having owned the property. That didn't mean she never lived there it simply meant that documentation wasn't held at the land registry.

Delighted as I was to receive the reply, so far as my research was concerned, it was like hitting another brick wall.

In a final attempt, I wrote to the Enquiries Department at Bromley Central Library to see if their Local History Department could turn up any information on the house, or the author. I received a most welcome reply from their Local Studies Library. They had searched through back copies of the Electoral Registers for the address advertised and found that in the 1930's a Leslie and Elizabeth COMPTON were living there. Magic! Just as Richmal had a paralysed **R**ight leg wanting for life, the Comptons had a surname wanting an **R** in their name if they were to fit into the author's family. The librarian queried whether this similarity of Compton and Crompton was where the confusion lay.

After everybody's hard work I was, in my own mind, satisfied that at last the mystery was solved, and I was able to write my story in time for the group's next meeting.

# 11 ~ MUM'S ROUTINE BLOOD PRESSURE CHECK-UP AT THE AGE OF 98

| | |
|---|---|
| Doctor | Good afternoon, Mrs Taylor. How are you today? |
| Mum | Well, doctor, it's this tumour at the back of my eye. It's sending pains right down into my foot. |
| | *(The doctor looked puzzled, and rapidly scanned the computer screen for a record of this).* |
| Doctor | What tumour is this, Mrs Taylor? I don't seem to know anything about a tumour! There's nothing on my computer about anything like that. |
| Janet | I think Mum's gone back about five years, doctor, to the time when I took her for an eye test and the optician said that the back of her eye was breaking up and there was nothing they could do about it because of her age. |
| Doctor | Let me check her medical records from the optician. |
| | *(Doctor disappeared and came back with a large medical file, which she thumbed through).* |
| | Oh, yes, you're right. That was in 1996. I see she had a cataract removed in the year 2000. |
| Janet | That's right, she did. |
| Doctor | Oh, Mrs Taylor, look at what your doctor said about you when he wrote to the hospital about removing your cataract. I'll read it to you: |
| | "This delightful lady and I are both of the opinion that she will reach 100 years of age." |
| Mum | What did he say? Read it to me again. |
| Doctor | THIS DELIGHTFUL LADY AND I ARE BOTH OF THE OPINION THAT SHE WILL REACH 100 YEARS OF AGE." |

| | |
|---|---|
| Mum | Oh, how lovely! What a clever doctor he was to think that! |
| | *(Mum's chest swelled with pride. A huge grin covered her face).* |
| Doctor | Well, Mrs Taylor, I don't think that the problem you've had with your eyes has anything to do with the pain in your foot. I think that's a different issue. How do you feel now? |
| Mum | Oh, I'm very well now doctor, after hearing the news that I'm probably going to live to be 100. It's just this pain that I get in my head. I think it's something to do with my blood pressure. When you're alone, you sit and think about things, and you imagine all sorts of things, don't you? |
| Doctor | Well, you came here today for a blood pressure check-up, so shall we do it now? Are you ready for me to take it? |
| Mum | Oh, yes. That's all right. I'm ready. |
| Doctor | I want you to sit still. Just relax and keep very quiet while I take it. |
| Mum | Yes, doctor, I know. I've had it done before. |
| | *(Doctor started the blood pressure test ..... 2 seconds elapsed).* |
| | Have you been on your holidays this year, doctor? |
| Doctor | Shush! Quiet now, Mrs Taylor, please don't talk. |
| Mum | Oh, you went to New York! Was it nice there? Did you enjoy it? |
| Doctor | Shsh! Please don't chatter just yet. |
| Mum | I'm sorry to hear it was wet. Didn't you get any good weather? It's awful here today. We got soaked just coming in from the car. |

| | |
|---|---|
| Doctor | Shsh, Mrs Taylor, please don't talk while the blood pressure machine is working. |
| Mum | Did it take you long to get there, doctor? Did you fly? |
| Doctor | Shush! Shsh! The machine needs you to be very quiet and still. |
| Mum | Oh, I am, doctor, I haven't said a word! |

*(Doctor raises her eyebrows but doesn't say anything, just finishes her procedure).*

Is my blood pressure still as good as it was the last time I came? A man doctor took it then.

| | |
|---|---|
| Doctor | You're in very good health, Mrs Taylor. The report from the blood test that was taken the last time you were here was excellent. Everything was very satisfactory, especially your kidneys, they're working 100%. |
| Mum | That's very good news. |
| Doctor | I'll just check your feet for you whilst you're here. |

*(Mum removed her shoes and stockings and the doctor examined both of her feet).*

You have a nasty callous on the soles of each foot. I'll make an appointment for a chiropodist to have a look at them for you.

| | |
|---|---|
| Mum | Thank you very much, doctor. When do you want to see me again? |
| Doctor | I'll see you in three months' time, for another check-up. |
| Mum | Oh dear, not for another three months? That's a long time! It takes us through to November. |
| Doctor | That's right. You can make an appointment with the receptionist on your way out. We'll see you again before Christmas. You'll probably have seen the |

|      |      |
|------|------|
|      | chiropodist by then and have had some treatment. Take care going home in the rain. Bye-bye. |
| Mum  | Thank you very much, doctor. Thank you. |

*(Outside the surgery, in the corridor, on the way to reception)*:

What a lovely lady. Isn't she wonderful? I feel so much better for coming. You can talk to her, and she will listen, not like the old folks in the home who only want to talk about themselves. **She** understands the art of good conversation!

# 12 ~ MY FIRST HIP OPERATION

Having been in excruciating pain for several months, the time had arrived when something had to be done about my left hip joint. My GP recommended having a replacement. I was very wary. I felt I was far too young. On the other hand, a younger relative than me had his first hip joint replaced when he was only twenty-eight years of age and eighteen years later had it replaced again; plus the one in his other hip, and coped so why was I frightened at the prospect?

The Surgeon was reassuring. My new joint would remove my current pain! I would be able to walk without limping! My mobility would improve because I wouldn't need to use a walking-stick so I would look younger and fitter! I decided to take his advice and had my name added to his waiting list.

The day came when I was admitted to hospital. Everyone there was caring. There were four beds in a side-ward off a long, larger ward. Opposite me there was a lady in need of a knee operation. The patient on her left, by the window, was due to have a hip-joint replacement. On my right a lady in her eighties was another knee patient. I was allocated a bed nearest to the door.

At midnight a nurse put up 'NIL BY MOUTH' notices above each of our beds as we were all to have our operations the next day. Lights were dimmed; but at first none of us could sleep. We chatted amongst ourselves until both the knee patients dozed off.

As I lay in this unfamiliar environment, wondering what I was letting myself in for, and how I would cope in the future, I could hear rustling and munching sounds coming from the bed near the window on the opposite side of the room. It was a struggle to raise myself in the bed to see what was happening, but eventually I did, and saw the other hip-patient selecting and eating chocolates from a huge box on her bed. I tried to advise her kindly:

"You're not supposed to eat anything just yet. We were told we couldn't even have a drink of water before our operations."

"I know. But I'm hungry," came the reply, and the chocolate chomping continued.

Next morning the youngest knee-op patient was taken away first. I was the last to go. When I woke up my husband was sitting by my bedside, and held my hand.

"You'll be all right now, love. It's all over," he assured.

The night-nibbler near the window was vomiting uncontrollably in her bed. The stench was abysmal. Nurses who attended her twice during visiting hour were not amused as they cleared the dark brown mess and changed her sheets.

Two days later it was my birthday. My husband brought an iced fruitcake and a sharp knife to cut it. A nurse made me a party hat out of a new, clean, upturned sputum bowl; took the ribbon from my gift of flowers to make a hatband, and inserted a flower in it. My husband lit the candle on the cake and they all sang "Happy Birthday to You." I blew out the candle and he shared the cake amongst us all.

Just after midnight that night I was woken from my sleep by the sound of screaming and shouting:

"Get out of my bed! Get away you pervert! Nurse. Nurse. Come quick. Come quick. There's a man – I can't move! Help! Help!"

With our newly-replaced hip and knee joints we couldn't move easily or quickly. We couldn't reach our bell-pushes to bring immediate help. In the dim light of the room I could see the shape of a man leaning over the chocoholic hip-op woman in the bed by the window. He appeared to be groping and trying to climb on top of her.

Panic set in when I suddenly remembered that my husband had forgotten to take the carving knife away and had left it on top of my locker. I thought the attacker might have found it and was trying to kill her. It took a lot of effort to raise my immobile body and turn it to look in the direction of my locker, but there I briefly saw a glint of steel.

'Oh, thank goodness he hasn't found it,' I thought. It hurt to reach over and hide it under a towel.

Lights went on. Shouting and confusion worsened. A nurse came in response to all the yelling and shouting. She ran across to the man and coaxed him off the terrified woman.

"Come along, Edward. You're in the wrong room. This isn't your ward-room; you should be in the next one along the corridor."

She persuasively led him back to his own bed, then came back and explained that he'd been to the lavatory and was surprised to find someone in his bed when he came back. He wasn't deliberately groping the patient; he was just trying to get back into what he thought was his own bed.

Each and everyone of us was in shock, but most of all the victim. We were all given hot sweet tea to settle us down. Next morning Edward was moved to recuperate in another hospital, and the hip patient was given a written apology.

Within a couple of weeks we were all discharged and although that was twelve years ago, I've never seen any of them again. I trust their operations were as successful as mine.

I look back now with gratitude at the skills and accomplishments of the medical teams who made my current life possible – pain-free and memorable. Unwittingly, they gave me the confidence to have my other hip joint replaced seven years later. On that occasion nothing so scary happened, but two days before my second hip operation, my Mum died in her centenary year. That is why I remember these events so clearly.